Windows® 95 Essentials
Level II

Ellen Colombo

Windows® 95 Essentials Level II

Copyright© 1996 by Que® Education & Training

All rights reserved. Printed in the United States of America. No part of this book may be used or reproduced in any form or by any means, or stored in a database or retrieval system, without prior written permission of the publisher except in the case of brief quotations embodied in critical articles and reviews. Making copies of any part of this book for any purpose other than your own personal use is a violation of United States copyright laws. For information, address Que Education & Training, Macmillan Computer Publishing, 201 W. 103rd Street, Indianapolis, IN 46290.

ISBN: 1-57576-255-2

This book is sold as is, without warranty of any kind, either express or implied, respecting the contents of this book, including but not limited to implied warranties for the book's quality, performance, merchantability, or fitness for any particular purpose. Neither Que Corporation nor its dealers or distributors shall be liable to the purchaser or any other person or entity with respect to any liability, loss, or damage caused or alleged to be caused directly or indirectly by this book.

99 98 97 96   4 3 2 1

Interpretation of the printing code: the rightmost double-digit number is the year of the book's printing; the rightmost single-digit number, the number of the book's printing. For example, a printing code of 96-1 shows that the first printing of the book occurred in 1996.

Screens reproduced in this book were created using Collage Plus from Inner Media, Inc., Hollis, NH.

President and Publisher: David P. Ewing

Publishing Director: Charles O. Stewart III

Product Marketing Manager: Susan J. Dollman

Acquisitions Editors: Rob Tidrow, Diane E. Beausoleil

Managing Editor: Jenny Watson

Production Editor: Theresa Mathias

Cover Designer: Ann Jones

Book Designer: Paula Carroll

Production Team: Mary Ann Abramson, Michael Brumitt, Charlotte Clapp, Terrie Deemer, Michael Dietsch, Jason Hand, Louisa Klucznik, Brian-Kent Proffitt, Laura Robbins, Bobbi Satterfield, Carol Sheehan, Laura Smith, SA Springer, Susan Van Ness, Mark Walchle, Todd Wente

Developed by Tim Huddleston

Technical review by Allan Wyatt

Composed in *Stone Serif* and *MCPdigital* by Que® Education & Training

About the Author

Ellen Colombo is an independent consultant in Manhattan, specializing in training investment banking personnel in the Wall Street area. Most recently, she trained personnel at Goldman Sachs Investment Banking Division in their conversion from the UNIX/Oracle environment to Windows NT/Office. In addition to teaching the Microsoft Office product suite and being certified in Word for Windows, she teaches a variety of other applications, most notably Windows 95, Windows NT, and Internet products.

Ellen is currently training Windows 95 and Internet courses to students through Systron, Inc., which is a Microsoft Solutions Provider Partner that is recognized by *LAN Magazine* as one of the top complex network integrators in America (LAN 100). Systron executives author many technical articles and white papers for business and trade publications, and are often quoted in the trade and popular press as industry experts.

Acknowledgments

To David Willey, who made this possible; and, of course, to Joey for his encouragement.

Trademark Acknowledgments

All terms mentioned in this book that are known to be trademarks or service marks have been appropriately capitalized. Que Education & Training cannot attest to the accuracy of this information. Use of a term in this book should not be regarded as affecting the validity of any trademark or service mark.

Microsoft and Windows are registered trademarks of Microsoft Corporation.

Preface

Que Education & Training is the educational publishing imprint of Macmillan Computer Publishing, the world's leading computer book publisher. Macmillan Computer Publishing books have taught more than 20 million people how to be productive with their computers.

This expertise in producing high-quality computer tutorial and reference books is evident in every Que Education & Training title we publish. The same tried-and-true authoring and product-development process that makes Macmillan Computer Publishing books best-sellers is used to ensure that training materials from Que Education & Training contain the most accurate and most up-to-date information. Experienced and respected software trainers write and review every manuscript to provide class-tested pedagogy. Quality-assurance editors check every keystroke and command in Que Education & Training books to ensure that instructions are clear and precise.

Above all, Macmillan Computer Publishing and, in turn, Que Education & Training have years of experience in meeting the learning demands of adult users in business and at home. We offer tiered courseware that

➤ provides broad-based, flexible training for novices through expert users

➤ is anchored in the practical and professional needs of adult learners

➤ includes trainer support in fully annotated *Instructor's Manuals*

The "Essentials" of Hands-On Learning

The *Essentials* of applications tutorials is appropriate for use in both corporate training and college classroom settings. The *Essentials Workbooks* are ideal for short courses—from a few hours to a full day or more—and meet the needs of adult learners. They can also be used effectively as computer-lab applications modules to accompany Que Education & Training's computer concepts text, *Computers in Your Future*, by Marilyn Meyer and Roberta Baber, both of Fresno City College; and *Using Computers and Information*, by Jack Rochester of Plymouth State College. The *Essentials Workbooks* enable users to become self-sufficient quickly; encourage self-learning after instruction; maximize learning through clear, complete explanations; and serve as future references. Each *Essentials* module is two-color throughout and sized at 8-1/2×11 inches for maximum screen-shot visibility. Each text contains a disk with the data files needed to complete the tutorials and end-of-chapter exercises.

Project Objectives list what learners will do and learn from the project.

"Why Would I Do This?" shows learners why this material is essential.

Step-by-Step Tutorials simplify the procedures with large screen shots, captions, and annotations.

If There's a Problem... anticipates common pitfalls and advises learners accordingly.

Inside Stuff provides tips and shortcuts for more effective applications.

Key Terms are highlighted in the text and defined in the margin when they first appear.

Jargon Watch offers a layperson's view of "technobabble" in easily understandable terms.

Applying Your Skills contains directed, hands-on exercises to check comprehension and reinforce learning.

Data Disks contain files for the text's step-by-step tutorials.

Instructor's Manual

If you have adopted this text for use in a college classroom, you will receive, upon request, an *Instructor's Manual* on disk at no additional charge. The manual contains suggested curriculum guides for courses of varying lengths, teaching tips, answers to exercises in the "Applying Your Skills" sections, test questions and answers, data files needed to complete each exercise, and solution files. Please contact your local representative or write to us on school letterhead at Macmillan Computer Publishing, 201 West 103rd Street, Indianapolis, IN 46290-1907, Attn: S. Dollman.

Also available is a printed *Instructor's Manual,* which is an ideal companion guide to workbooks in the *Essentials* series. It includes teaching concepts and procedures, strategies for structuring content and organizing the class, ideas for adapting the material for various audiences, pre-training assessment and post-class evaluation tools, and much more. The backbone of the *Instructor's Manual* is a heavily annotated student workbook that serves as an indispensable resource for trainers. New instructors will appreciate the tips that help them teach a topic successfully for the first time. Experienced trainers will appreciate fresh approaches to teaching familiar topics.

Que Education & Training
Publishing for tomorrow...*today*

Table of Contents at a Glance

Project 1   **Personalizing Windows 95** 1

Project 2   **Using Microsoft Exchange** 29

Project 3   **Printing, Modems, and Faxing** 51

Project 4   **Getting the Most from Windows 95 Help** 79

Project 5   **Introduction to Networks** 99

Project 6   **Using the Briefcase** 117

Project 7   **Accessing The Microsoft Network** 131

Index 153

Table of Contents

Project 1 Personalizing Windows 95   1
Lesson 1: Customizing the Taskbar 2
Lesson 2: Adding Shortcuts to the Desktop 5
Lesson 3: Adding an Item to the Start Menu 8
Lesson 4: Removing Items from the Start Menu 12
Lesson 5: Setting How a Program Opens 14
Lesson 6: Managing Documents in the Start Menu 17
Lesson 7: Customizing My Computer 19
Lesson 8: Working with Fonts 21
Lesson 9: Securing Your Desktop 25

            Project Summary 27
            Applying Your Skills 28

Project 2 Using Microsoft Exchange   29
Lesson 1: Accessing Mail through Microsoft Exchange 30
Lesson 2: Creating New Folders in Microsoft Exchange 33
Lesson 3: Setting Preferences in Microsoft Exchange 35
Lesson 4: Creating and Sending Mail Messages 39
Lesson 5: Reading and Replying to Mail Messages 44
Lesson 6: Adding a Name to Your Personal Address Book 46

            Project Summary 49
            Applying Your Skills 50

Project 3 Printing, Modems, and Faxing   51
Lesson 1: Setting Up a Printer 52
Lesson 2: Setting Up a Modem 56
Lesson 3: Using HyperTerminal to Connect to a
                 Remote Computer 59
Lesson 4: Setting Up Your Fax 62
Lesson 5: Sending a Fax 65
Lesson 6: Receiving Faxes 67
Lesson 7: Working With Dial-Up Networking 72
Lesson 8: Using Phone Dialer 76

            Project Summary 77
            Applying Your Skills 78

Project 4 Getting the Most from Windows 95 Help   79
Lesson 1: Finding a Topic in Help 80
Lesson 2: Browsing Help for Similar Topics 86
Lesson 3: Copying Information from a Help Topic 87
Lesson 4: Printing a Help Topic 89
Lesson 5: Adding Comments to Help Topics 91
Lesson 6: How to Get Help in a Dialog Box 93
Lesson 7: Changing the Font Size of a Help Topic 95
Lesson 8: Changing System Colors in a Help Topic 96

            Project Summary 98
            Applying Your Skills 98

Project 5   Introduction to Networks   **99**

    Lesson 1: Finding a Computer on a Network 100

    Lesson 2: Browsing Your Workgroup 103

    Lesson 3: Sharing Folders, Files, and Printers on a Network 106

    Lesson 4: Printing and Troubleshooting Network Issues 109

    Lesson 5: Connecting to Remote Networks 110

    Lesson 6: Connecting to a Remote Machine Not Using
Windows 95 113

    Project Summary 115

    Applying Your Skills 115

Project 6   Using the Briefcase   **117**

    Lesson 1: Preparing Two Computers to Use the Briefcase 118

    Lesson 2: Creating a New Briefcase in the Explorer 122

    Lesson 3: Copying Files to a New Briefcase in the Explorer 124

    Lesson 4: Returning Briefcase Files to the Main Computer 126

    Lesson 5: Using the Briefcase with Floppy Disks 127

    Project Summary 129

    Applying Your Skills 130

Project 7   Accessing The Microsoft Network   **131**

    Lesson 1: Accessing MSN and Seeing What It Offers 133

    Lesson 2: Navigating Categories and Member Assistance 138

    Lesson 3: Downloading a File from MSN 141

    Lesson 4: Accessing and Using Chat Rooms 144

    Lesson 5: Accessing and Using Bulletin Board Services 147

    Lesson 6: Browsing Internet Newsgroups 148

    Lesson 7: Disconnecting from The Microsoft Network 149

    Project Summary 150

    Applying Your Skills 151

Index   **153**

Note to the Learner

Welcome to the *Windows 95 Essentials Level II* workbook! The *Essentials* series consists of student workbooks and instructor manuals for use in instructor-led classes.

If this is your first experience with instructor-led training, you're in for a real treat. Instructor-led, hands-on training is the fastest and most efficient means of teaching software applications. Your instructor is an expert in this application, so he/she can answer your questions and pass on valuable advice about using the software.

What all this means is that with the use of these materials, you'll be up and running in the shortest amount of time possible.

Who Should Use This Book?

The *Essentials* workbooks are designed to be used in the classroom and corporate-training environment. The projects in the *Essentials* workbooks are designed to teach only the "bare essentials"—just enough for you to get the job done.

How To Use This Book

Because an instructor will be present in the classroom, the *Essentials* workbooks contain a minimum of explanation and the maximum of step-by-step directions. As you begin each project, you are told what you want to accomplish and why. Realistic examples are given, so that you can quickly relate to the task and see the value of completing the project.

Each project is a series of separate lessons with detailed instructions to guide you through the completion of a task. After each numbered step, a brief explanation of the action is given to help you really understand "why you just did that." At the end of each lesson, tips and shortcuts are given to satisfy the more curious reader. A Project Summary table is included to give you a quick reference to sue when you need a quick refresher.

To make your learning experience as enjoyable as possible, the projects are task-oriented and use real-world business examples.

Task-Oriented Lessons

The workbook lessons are *task-oriented*, which means that you actually accomplish a task as you work through the lesson. For example, rather than merely *reading* about moving and copying text, you learn how to rearrange your text by moving and copying sentences in a paragraph. Likewise, you learn how to format documents by changing the margins, changing the line spacing, setting justification, changing the font and font size, and adding page numbers and a header.

Once you get past the first two projects, the remainder are independent of each other—they can be completed in any order. If your time is limited, you can pick and choose your projects, depending on which concepts you need to learn right away.

Real-World Examples

Concepts are illustrated with realistic situations that you would encounter in a workplace. The more realistic the examples are, the easier it is for you to relate to the situation. For example, in the lesson in which you complete a newsletter, the sample file contains information that you would find in a typical corporate newsletter. You work with letters to conference attendees, status reports, annual reports, and job descriptions instead of letters to book clubs or public-domain documents (such as the Declaration of Independence).

Conventions Used in This Book

The *Essentials* series uses the following conventions to make it easier for you to understand the material:

➤ Text that you are to type appears in **color and boldface**

➤ Underlined letters in menu names, menu commands, and dialog-box options appear in a different color. Examples are the File menu, the Open command, and the File name list box.

➤ Important words or phrases appear in *italic* the first time they are discussed.

➤ *Key terms* are defined in the margin as soon as they are introduced.

➤ On-screen text and messages appear in a `special font`.

➤ *If you have problems...* boxes contain troubleshooting tips that anticipate common pitfalls. These are designed to help you solve your own problems so that you can keep up with the rest of the class.

➤ *Jargon Watch* boxes are used to define a group of key terms used in the project.

➤ *Inside Stuff* boxes contain tips and shortcuts to help you use the application more effectively.

Project 1

1

Personalizing Windows 95

Objectives

In this project, you learn how to

➤ Customize the Taskbar

➤ Add Shortcuts to the Desktop

➤ Add an Item to the Start Menu

➤ Remove Items from the Start Menu

➤ Set How a Program Opens

➤ Manage Documents in the Start Menu

➤ Customize My Computer

➤ Work with Fonts

➤ Secure Your Desktop

Why Would I Do This?

n this project, you build on the basic ways to personalize Windows 95 that were discussed in *Windows 95 On the Job Essentials, Level I.* You learned how to change your screen saver, wallpaper, and other basic interfaces in Level I. In this project, you learn how to personalize the Windows desktop and save time by having only those items you use handy, automating routine tasks, and creating shortcuts on your desktop so you don't have to search for files and tools you frequently use.

This project shows you how to customize your Taskbar to work the way you want it to, personalize your Start menu and desktop for quick access to items you use regularly, control your fonts and display fonts, and make your desktop more secure. Throughout this project, you'll get some inside tips and shortcuts to help you master the new environment.

Lesson 1: Customizing the Taskbar

The best place to start personalizing Windows is by customizing your Taskbar. Because the Taskbar is the central location of all your open applications, files, and tools, you are going to want to make your Taskbar reflect your own routines and habits. You might want to have the Taskbar visible at all times, or you might want to see it only when you need to use it. The default setting in Windows 95 is for large icons to appear on the Start menu. You might decide to change this setting for a smaller, less intrusive Start menu. Or you might want a clock on your Taskbar to keep track of the time. Then again, you might want to turn it off so you aren't reminded the day is dragging! Try the steps now to make your Taskbar act the way you want it to.

To Customize the Taskbar

❶ Turn your computer on.

Your company policy might be to leave computers on at all times, or you might not be able to carry out this first step. If the computer is already on, proceed to step 2.

❷ Type in your user ID and your password.

Most corporations use a system of user identification and passwords to provide a way of telling the network who you are, and that it should look for the setup you are used to seeing when you log on. Windows 95 launches automatically after your user ID and password are verified, unless your Systems Administrator specified that another program should begin before Windows 95 launches.

Lesson 1: Customizing the Taskbar   3

③ Click the Start button on the Taskbar.

You can perform diverse tasks directly from the Start button in Windows 95. The Start button on the Taskbar is also the fastest way to access Help.

④ Click Settings.

The dark arrow pointing to the right from the Settings option tells you that Windows has more options for you to choose from in that menu item. Those options appear on the Settings fly-out menu, as shown in Figure 1.1.

Figure 1.1
You can open and locate any item from the Start button.

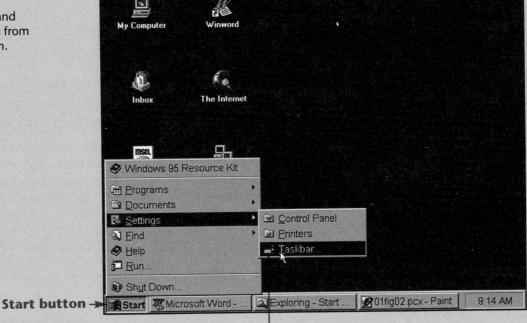

Start button →

Choose Taskbar to customize settings for the Start menu and the Taskbar

⑤ Click Taskbar.

The Settings menu provides an easy way to customize the Taskbar. You can also adjust Control Panel settings and Printer settings from the Settings menu. The Taskbar Properties dialog box appears and opens to the Taskbar Options tab, as shown in Figure 1.2.

continues

4 Project 1 Personalizing Windows 95

To Customize the Taskbar (continued)

Figure 1.2
Set Taskbar Properties to your preferences in this dialog box.

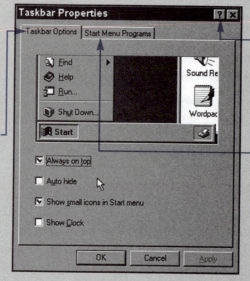

Personalize Taskbar options on this tab

Click this question mark, then click any item on the current tab for help with that item

Personalize Start menu options on this tab

6 **Click to select the Show Clock option, then click Apply.**

View the Taskbar. This option makes the clock visible in the right corner of your Taskbar. If you rest your cursor over the time, the date appears. If you right-click the time, you can select the option in the shortcut menu to Adjust Date/Time. If you later decide you don't want to see the clock, you can clear the Show Clock check box to deselect that option.

Notice the question mark in the upper-right corner of the dialog box. If you need help with any item, click the question mark, then click the item you want help on. A help box appears, explaining more about the item.

You can move the Taskbar to any border of your desktop. Windows 95 defaults with the Taskbar located at the bottom of your desktop, but you can move it to the left, right, or top margin of your screen.

If the Taskbar does not display all the items you currently have open, you can rest your cursor over the edge of the Taskbar. A double-headed arrow appears to allow you to grab the edge of the Taskbar and enlarge it if you need to.

Lesson 2:   Adding Shortcuts to the Desktop   **5**

7 **Select the Show Small Icons in Start Menu check box and click Apply.**

Click the Start Menu. You can see the smaller menu and icons listed on the Start menu. If you prefer the larger icons, click to deselect the option. Each option on the Taskbar Options tab toggles on if there is a check mark in the box to the left of the option, and toggles off if the check box is clear. Clicking in the box toggles the option on and off.

8 **Select the Auto Hide check box and click Apply.**

When you do this, you don't see the Taskbar on your screen. Instead, you see a thin gray line on the edge of the location where the Taskbar resides. If you need to use the Taskbar, move your cursor toward the gray line, and the Taskbar appears.

9 **Select the Always on Top check box and click Apply.**

Selecting this option keeps the Taskbar on top of applications that are visible on your screen.

10 **Click OK.**

The Taskbar Properties dialog box closes.

Lesson 2: Adding Shortcuts to the Desktop

Windows 95 lets you save time by creating shortcuts; the items you need are always immediately available from the desktop or a folder. A shortcut provides immediate access to any application, file, or printer you frequently use. These shortcuts free you from drilling through menus, submenus, lists, and dialog boxes to open an item. You can place a shortcut on the desktop or in any folder.

In this lesson, you add a calculator to your desktop so it is available with a double-click if you need to quickly perform any mathematical functions. The following steps show you how to create a shortcut.

To Add a Shortcut to Your Desktop

1 **Right-click the Start button.**

The shortcut menu appears, as shown in Figure 1.3. You will use the Explore option in this lesson. In addition to opening the Explorer, you can open the Start Menu folder by clicking Open, or you can click Find to find any files or folders on your computer.

continues

6 Project 1   Personalizing Windows 95

To Add a Shortcut to Your Desktop   (continued)

Figure 1.3
Right-click the Start button to provide more file access and assistance options.

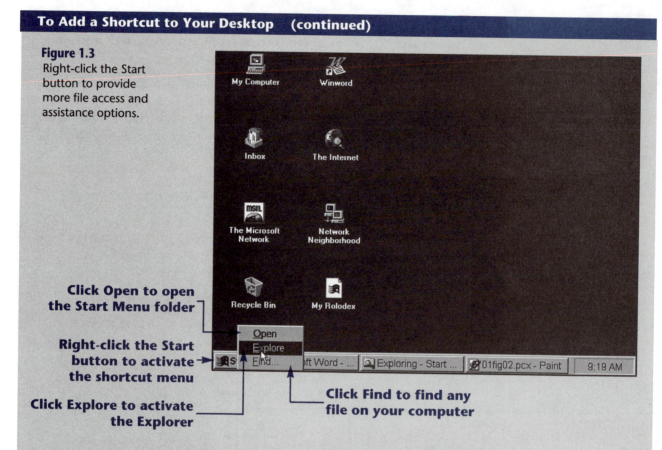

Click Open to open the Start Menu folder

Right-click the Start button to activate the shortcut menu

Click Explore to activate the Explorer

Click Find to find any file on your computer

2 **Click Explore now to open the Explorer.**

Explorer opens. Explorer is quite similar to My Computer. The main difference between the way the two function is that the Explorer has two panels, while My Computer has one full screen. With the Explorer, you can work with files between the left and right panels separately.

3 **Click the word Windows in the left panel of the Explorer.**

Generally, the left panel shows the folders available on your computer. The right panel displays the contents of the currently selected folder (see Fig. 1.4).

If you have problems...

Computers are frequently configured differently. You might not see Windows as a folder in the left panel of Explorer. If you do not see the Windows folder, ask your instructor what file you should use for this exercise.

Lesson 2:   Adding Shortcuts to the Desktop

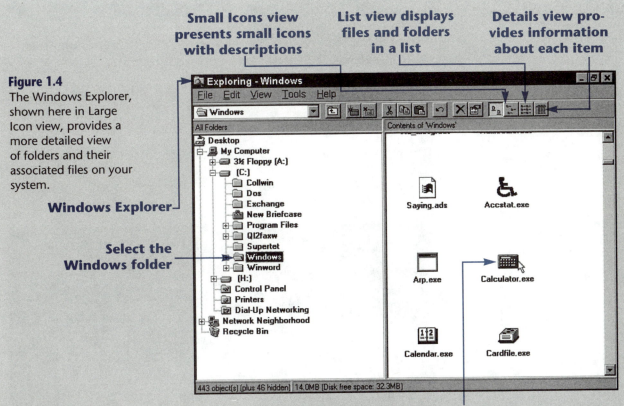

Figure 1.4
The Windows Explorer, shown here in Large Icon view, provides a more detailed view of folders and their associated files on your system.

Small Icons view presents small icons with descriptions

List view displays files and folders in a list

Details view provides information about each item

Select the Windows folder

Scroll to find the Calculator—it might be listed as Calc or as a large icon with a descriptive name

4 Scroll in the right panel to find the CALCULATOR.EXE icon.

Your screen should be in Normal view, so some desktop space is showing. The view might differ from Figure 1.4, depending on your view choice. If you are in Details view, you can locate a file in Explorer by clicking once on the word Name above the file names in the Name column. This sorts the files by their file name, in ascending order. You can click Name again to reverse to descending order.

5 Click to select the calculator file icon.

Press Ctrl+Shift and drag the Calculator icon or the descriptive term to your desktop. You can drag it to any location on the desktop. Notice the cursor shows a copy of the calculator icon and name as you drag.

6 Release the mouse button, then release the Ctrl+Shift keys.

A shortcut menu appears. You can use this menu to move or copy files, or to create a shortcut to a file, printer, or application.

continues

Project 1 Personalizing Windows 95

To Add a Shortcut to Your Desktop (continued)

⑦ **Click Create Shortcut(s) Here to create the shortcut on your desktop. Figure 1.5 shows the options available.**

The Calculator shortcut icon is available on your desktop. Double-click to view the Calculator now.

⑧ **Click the Close button on the Calculator.**

This will close the Calculator in preparation for the next lesson.

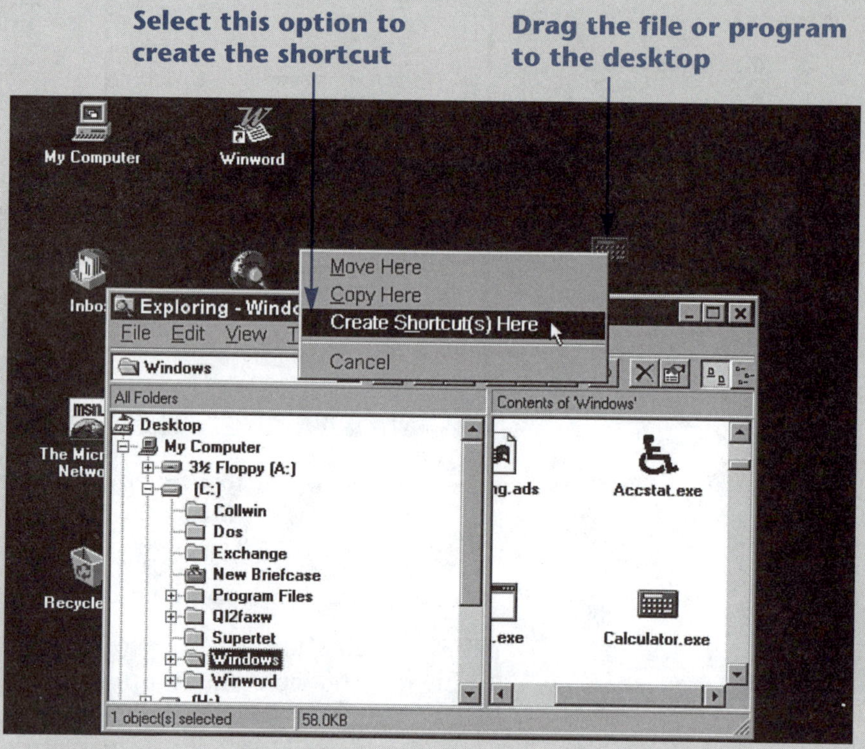

Figure 1.5
Placing an item on the Desktop is easy with drag and drop.

Select this option to create the shortcut

Drag the file or program to the desktop

You can even put just a part of a document on your desktop. For example, you might want to take a table of available flights out of a memo regarding current travel plans, but you aren't yet ready to begin your letter of response. Just select the text or graphic you want to copy and drag it to anywhere on your desktop. It becomes an icon on the desktop identified as a document scrap showing an abbreviated name.

Whenever you need it, drag it to the location where you want to insert it in a document and release the mouse button. You must be using an OLE-compliant application. Check with your instructor or Systems Administrator if you have any trouble.

Lesson 3: Adding an Item to the Start Menu

The Windows drag-and-drop capability provides an easy way to get a program or file onto your desktop, as you learned in Lesson 2. But you might not want to clutter your desktop with icons.

Lesson 3: Adding an Item to the Start Menu

Because you already access so many items directly through the Start button, you might want to add items directly to the Start button so you have one location for everything you need. Wordpad is a word processor program that is handy to have on the Start menu, so try the following steps to add Wordpad to your Start menu in case you need to quickly edit a document.

To Add an Item to the Start Menu

❶ Click the Start button on the Taskbar and select Settings, Taskbar.

Remember, you can also adjust **C**ontrol Panel settings and **P**rinter settings from here. The Taskbar Properties dialog box appears (refer to Figure 1.2).

❷ Click the Start Menu Programs tab.

From this tab, you control what items appear on the Start Menu.

❸ Click Add.

The Create Shortcut wizard appears (see Fig. 1.6). This wizard helps you build a shortcut by browsing for the item you want to add. The wizard asks you questions and leads you through the steps to create a shortcut on your Start menu.

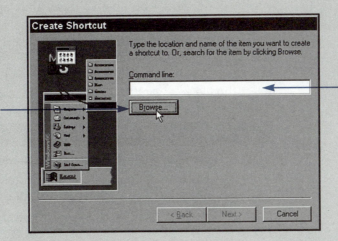

Figure 1.6
The Create Shortcut wizard allows you to customize items on your Start menu.

To locate an item you want to add, click here

If you know the item name and location, type it in this text box

❹ Click Browse.

The Browse dialog box opens (see Fig. 1.7). Select the **Program Files** folder.

❺ Click Open.

Select **Accessories**.

❻ Click Open.

Select **Wordpad** as your shortcut file to copy. Notice when you click to select the item, the item name and path appear in the File **N**ame box.

continues

10 Project 1 Personalizing Windows 95

To Add an Item to the Start Menu (continued)

Figure 1.7
Follow the Wizard to add items to your Start menu.

Browse to find Wordpad

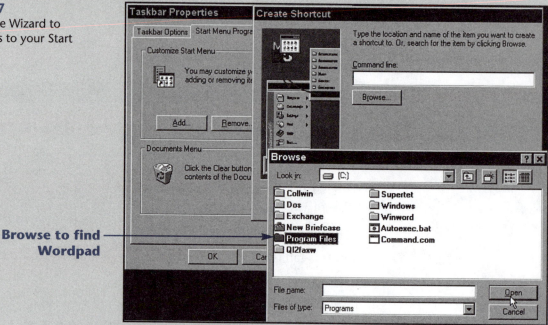

In this exercise, you are adding an application to the Start menu. When you're done, you'll be able to open that application from the Start menu and work on any document compatible with Wordpad. But don't forget that you can add a frequently used file directly to the Start menu, too. When you are in the Browse dialog box, click the drop-down arrow of the Files of Type list box and select All Files. Browse to select the file you want to put on the Start menu.

If you have problems...

You might have a different file setup than the standard Windows 95 file structure. If you do not see Programs as an option, or the Accessories folder, you can copy any file to use in this exercise. You'll learn how to delete it from the menu in the next exercise.

7 Click Open.

When you click Open, the Browse dialog box closes and you return to the Create Shortcut dialog box. The **C**ommand Line text box has the same file name and path that was listed in the File **N**ame text box of the Browse dialog box.

To save time when you are browsing, you can double-click the file or folder. This selects the item, places it in the File **N**ame text box and selects the **O**pen button to close the Browse dialog box and return to the Create Shortcut dialog box.

Also, if you know the full correct path name, you can type it in the **C**ommand Line text box in the Create Shortcut dialog box—and avoid browsing altogether.

Lesson 3: Adding an Item to the Start Menu

8 **Click the Next button in the Create Shortcut dialog box.**

The Wizard continues by displaying the Select Program Folder screen, where you select a folder to put your shortcut in.

9 **Click to select the Start menu folder (see Fig. 1.8).**

In this exercise, you'll put Wordpad in the Start Menu folder, but you can put new items you add later wherever you want them. You can also click New Folder if you want to create a new folder to place the shortcut in, and name it.

Figure 1.8
You can click to select the menu you want to place your item on.

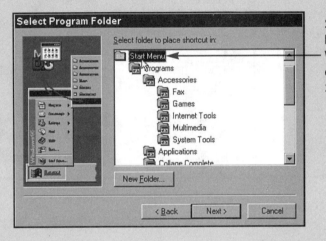

Select Start Menu to add Wordpad directly to the Start menu

10 **Click Next.**

The Wizard continues to the next screen. Select a Title for the Program. This screen allows you to change the way your Start menu displays the program name, if you want.

11 **Type the name you want to appear on the menu, then click Finish. You return to the Taskbar Properties dialog box.**

12 **Click OK to close the dialog box.**

Check the Start menu to verify that the new shortcut is where you want it. Repeat this procedure on your computer when you are at your desk to have all items you want handy placed where you need them. Figure 1.9 shows you that Wordpad is now located directly on the Start menu.

If you have problems...

You might get a prompt from Windows 95 asking you to choose an icon. If this happens, click to select an option, then click Finish at the prompt.

continues

Project 1 Personalizing Windows 95

To Add an Item to the Start Menu (continued)

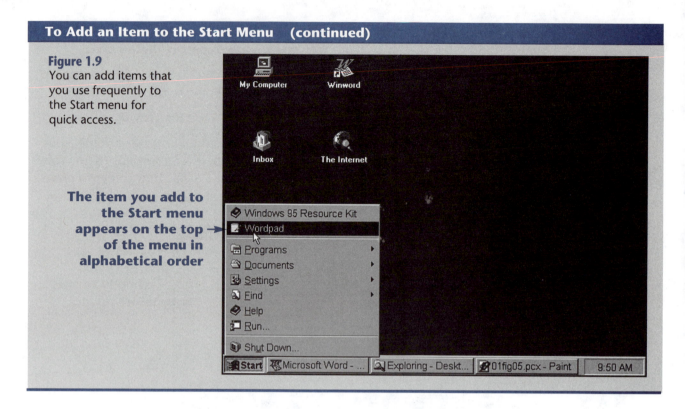

Figure 1.9
You can add items that you use frequently to the Start menu for quick access.

The item you add to the Start menu appears on the top of the menu in alphabetical order

Lesson 4: Removing Items from the Start Menu

Now that you have added an item to your Start menu, you might already be thinking of ways you want to rearrange the way you access your work. In the next exercise, you learn how to remove items from the Start menu so the items appear in the order you prefer.

To Remove Items from the Start Menu

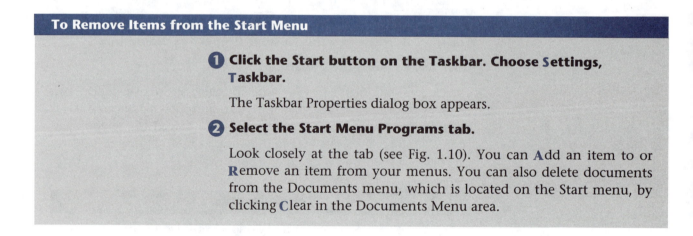

1 Click the Start button on the Taskbar. Choose **S**ettings, **T**askbar.

The Taskbar Properties dialog box appears.

2 Select the Start Menu Programs tab.

Look closely at the tab (see Fig. 1.10). You can **A**dd an item to or **R**emove an item from your menus. You can also delete documents from the Documents menu, which is located on the Start menu, by clicking **C**lear in the Documents Menu area.

Lesson 4: Removing Items from the Start Menu   13

Figure 1.10
Use the Start Menu Programs tab to make your desktop more efficient.

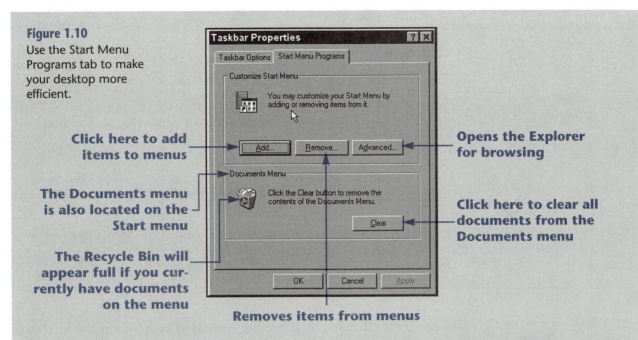

Click here to add items to menus

The Documents menu is also located on the Start menu

The Recycle Bin will appear full if you currently have documents on the menu

Opens the Explorer for browsing

Click here to clear all documents from the Documents menu

Removes items from menus

❸ Click Remove.

The Remove Shortcuts/Folders dialog box opens so you can select the item you want to remove (see Fig. 1.11).

Figure 1.11
Use the Remove Shortcuts/Folders dialog box to delete items from the Start menu.

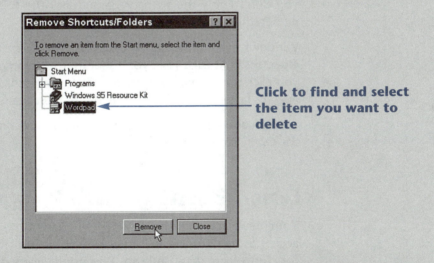

Click to find and select the item you want to delete

❹ Select the Start Menu and scroll down the folder hierarchy tree using the scroll bar until you see Wordpad.

Each folder can contain a submenu. Double-click to open a folder containing submenus.

❺ Select Wordpad.

This activates the Remove button.

continues

14 Project 1 Personalizing Windows 95

> **To Remove Items from the Start Menu (continued)**
>
> **6 Click Remove.**
>
> This does not remove Wordpad from your computer, only from the Start menu.
>
> **7 Choose Close to return to the Taskbar Properties dialog box, then click OK.**
>
> The item is now off your menu.
>
> **8 Repeat the steps in Lesson 3 to add Wordpad to your menu again.**
>
> In the next lesson, you control how your Wordpad application opens, so make sure you add Wordpad back to your Start menu at this time.

Day-to-day users often miss out on the timesaving tip of using the Run command. If you don't want an item on your Start menu, but you want to quickly open a program or file, use **R**un. Click the Start button and choose **R**un.

In the Run dialog box that appears, type the correct name and path of the file, program, or document you want, click OK, and Windows will get it for you. If you don't know the path or name, click the **B**rowse button and locate your item in the familiar Browse dialog box.

Windows even saves past recent requests. Click the drop-down arrow of the **O**pen list box. Each time you use Run, the command is retained in a list. When you click the arrow, you can choose from recent past items you have requested—it's faster than typing in the information again.

You can also connect to a shared computer on a network by typing the path in the Open list box and clicking OK.

Lesson 5: Setting How a Program Opens

Your newly customized desktop will save time every day, allowing you to access things quickly from your Start button. But you need one more tool for controlling your desktop. You might want to open some applications to a minimized setting, while yought need to open others to their full size. In this lesson, you learn how to set items to open in either full-screen mode or as an icon on your Taskbar.

Lesson 5: Setting How a Program Opens

To Set How a Program Opens

❶ Right-click the Start button, then select Open.

The Start Menu window opens. Items located on the Start Menu window are visible as icons with labels. You can control settings for files and programs from this window.

❷ Right-click the Wordpad icon (see Fig. 1.12).

The shortcut menu appears.

Figure 1.12
You can control how each item on the Start menu opens.

Click Properties to view Wordpad properties

❸ Select Properties.

You can also select Properties from the File menu instead of right-clicking the Wordpad icon. The Wordpad Properties dialog box appears. You see two tabs: General and Shortcut.

❹ Click the Shortcut tab.

You can control many settings through this tab. You can change the icon that represents the item, or create a shortcut key for quick opening of the selected item.

❺ Click the drop-down arrow of the Run list box.

A drop-down list appears, offering several choices.

❻ The current selection is Normal Window. Select Maximized.

This sets the feature to open in a full screen. Figure 1.13 shows the drop-down list.

continues

Project 1 Personalizing Windows 95

To Set How a Program Opens (continued)

Figure 1.13
Use the Run list box to control how your Start menu programs open.

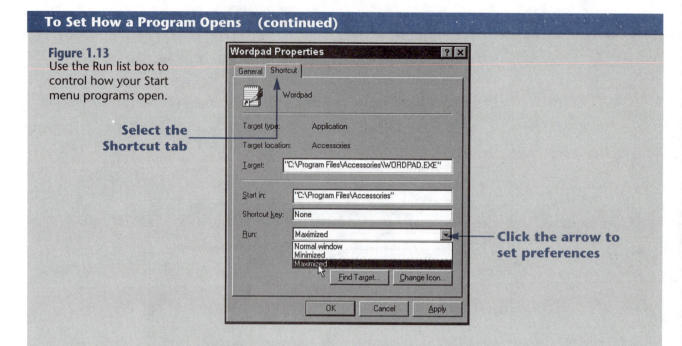

⑦ **Click OK.**

Refer to the preceding steps to control all the items you use most frequently, so they will open and be available to you with your preferences to save time.

⑧ **Close the Start Menu window.**

You can either click the Close button on the title bar or click File from the menu and select Close.

⑨ **Click the Start menu button.**

Select Wordpad and view how it opens to a full screen. Type your name in the screen. Remember how you type your name—you will locate this document later using this text as the search key.

⑩ **Click File, select Save, type name in the File Name text box and click Save.**

You will use this new file in the next exercise.

⑪ **Close Wordpad by clicking the Close button on the title bar or clicking File, Close. All files and dialog boxes should be closed.**

Lesson 6: Managing Documents in the Start Menu

You will often work on the same documents repeatedly over a period of time. Windows 95 recognizes most people's work patterns, and has provided a feature on the Start menu to help you access those documents quickly. When you no longer need the documents, you can clear the feature to start again. Use the steps in the next section to become familiar with an immediate way to access recently used documents.

To Manage Documents in the Start Menu

1 Click the Start button on the Taskbar.

This time you will be using another feature of the Start menu, **D**ocuments.

2 Select Documents.

A list of recently used documents appears to the right in a fly-out menu, as shown in Figure 1.14.

3 Click the document NAME.DOC in the fly-out menu to select it.

The Wordpad document you saved as name opens.

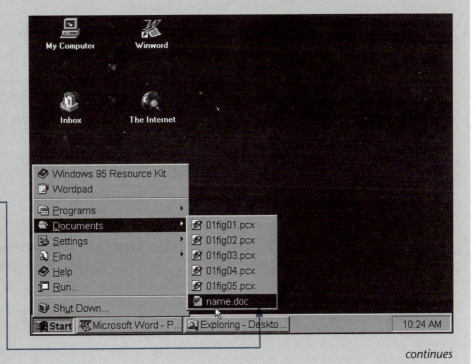

Figure 1.14
If you use documents frequently, save time by opening them from the Documents menu.

Recently used documents appear on the Documents menu

continues

To Manage Documents in the Start Menu (continued)

4 Close Wordpad.

When you are finished using a document, you will want to remove it from the Start menu. This does not delete the document. Try doing that in the next few steps.

5 Click the Start button and select Settings, Taskbar.

The Taskbar Properties dialog box appears.

6 Click the Start Menu Programs tab if it is not already selected.

The Document Menu area is located at the bottom of the Start Menu Programs tab. Refer to Figure 1.10 for a view of the Start Menu Programs tab if you need to.

7 Click the Clear button.

This clears the contents of the Documents menu.

8 Click OK.

This closes the Taskbar Properties dialog box and clears all documents currently on the Documents menu. Remember to clear your Document menu when you no longer need most of the documents on that menu.

9 Click the Start button.

10 Select Documents and view the fly-out menu. The word Empty appears grayed out in parenthesis.

If you have problems...

When you select **D**ocuments, you might find that the document sidebar is currently empty. The word Empty appears (grayed out) in parenthesis. Generally, this means you have not yet used a document or that you have recently cleared the Documents menu. However, it could also mean that your documents are created in the older 16-bit environment, as opposed to 32 bit. See the upcoming "Jargon Watch" to learn about the difference between the two. If you are still using 16-bit applications, such as Word for Windows 6.0, any document you open in the application will not appear on the Documents menu.

You can work around this limitation and show the file or document by opening it in the Explorer instead of in the 16-bit application. The next time you need the document, you can open it through the Documents menu.

Lesson 7: Customizing My Computer   19

Jargon Watch

The terms **16-bit environment** and **32-bit environment** sound highly technical, and to be sure, to those who have an interest, many hours can be spent studying these two computing architectures. But the relevance of these environments to your day-to-day world is minimal.

All you really need to understand is that the newer, 32-bit environment provides greater stability, meaning that your system is less likely to freeze up, or "crash." You also don't have to restart your computer if one running application becomes unstable, because each application runs separately from others. Older, 16-bit applications, on the other hand, don't operate independently of one another—so one application can affect the others if it becomes unstable.

Lesson 7: Customizing My Computer

You learned how to manage files and folders in My Computer in Level I. In this project, you have learned how to organize your desktop so that what you need is immediately available. You can tailor My Computer even further than you learned in Level I to complement the preferences you have on your desktop.

To Customize My Computer

1 Double-click My Computer on your Desktop.

My Computer is an easy way to see what is on your computer. You can also open My Computer by right-clicking My Computer and selecting **O**pen from the shortcut menu. Remember, you only have to double-click an icon to look at the drive you want. Each time you double-click, a new window opens.

You can press the Backspace key to move up one level from the currently selected folder.

Is your toolbar visible? If you don't see it, click **V**iew, and select **T**oolbar.

Remember from Level I, use the options on the View menu to change how your files display.

If you have problems...

You might find that your screen differs from the examples given in the book. You might be looking for a file that is on someone else's computer on a network. If this is the case, ask your instructor for assistance. Your instructor might tell you to double-click the Network Neighborhood icon rather than My Computer. Further instructions for Network Neighborhood are provided in Project 5 of this book.

continues

To Customize My Computer   (continued)

② Click View.

As Figure 1.15 shows, the View menu allows you to make the toolbar and status bar available if it isn't currently visible. The status bar explains the purpose of menu items as you click and pause over them during the selection process.

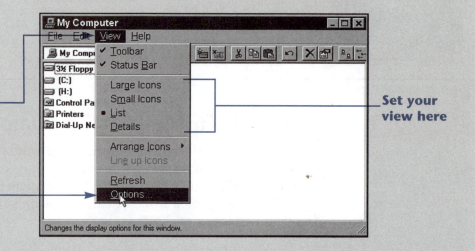

Figure 1.15
The View menu provides tools to customize My Computer.

Use the View menu to make the toolbar visible

Select Options to set My Computer to one screen to save system resources

Set your view here

③ Select Options.

The Options dialog box appears.

④ Click the Folder tab.

Options you set here are important tools for how system resources are handled and how you view your files. You are presented with the option to choose between having a new window open when you browse through each folder, or having the same window change. Every time you open a window, you use more systems resources. It is a good habit to use one window whenever possible to save resources.

⑤ Click the Browse Folders by Using a Single Window that Changes as You Open Each Folder button (see Fig. 1.16).

A graphic example of the view of each possible option is depicted on the tab to assist you while deciding which method you prefer to use.

Lesson 8: Working with Fonts

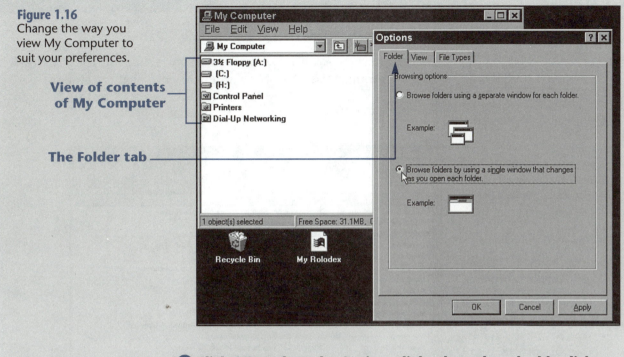

Figure 1.16
Change the way you view My Computer to suit your preferences.

View of contents of My Computer

The Folder tab

6 Click **OK** to close the Options dialog box, then double-click drive C: in My Computer.

Notice that a new window does not open. Instead, the new screen replaces the old screen. This saves systems resources so your computer can perform better.

7 Click **V**iew, **O**ptions, and click the Folder tab of the Options dialog box.

8 Click the Browse Folders Using a **S**eparate Window for Each Folder button.

Now when you use My Computer, a new window will open each time you double-click an icon. If you want to return it to view a separate window for each folder, repeat the steps and select the button Browse Folders by Using a Si**n**gle Window that Changes as You Open Each Folder.

Lesson 8: Working with Fonts

In the past, even with Windows 3.1 or Windows for Workgroups 3.11, there have been limitations when dealing with fonts. Windows 95 provides enhanced TrueType fonts and ways to view them prior to using them to maximize the effectiveness of the documents and presentations you create.

You can even adjust your icon fonts on your desktop with greater ease to minimize the strain on your eyes, or just to make your desktop more pleasing to your eye. Follow the steps in this lesson to familiarize yourself with the font options available in Windows 95.

To Work with Fonts

1 **Click Start and choose Settings, Control Panel.**

This is where you will make most property settings in the Windows 95 environment. Some options might be disabled by systems personnel for security reasons. Figure 1.17 shows the Control Panel in Details view to indicate the purpose of each item.

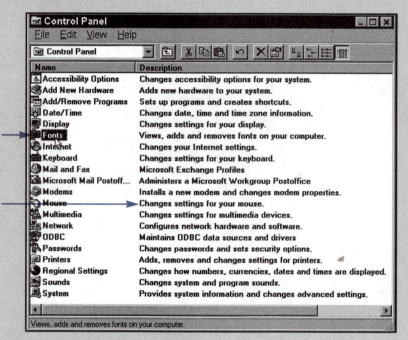

Figure 1.17
Use Control Panel in Details view to see a description of the purpose of each item.

Double-click to open an item's window

Each item controls specific hardware and software in Windows 95

2 **Double-click the Fonts folder.**

The Fonts folder opens, revealing all the fonts available to you. Now you can see what each font looks like.

3 **Double-click Arial.**

A dialog box appears, displaying the font in various sizes, as shown in Figure 1.18.

4 **Click Done when you are finished viewing the font to return to the Fonts folder.**

You can click Print if you want to print the font sample. You can also find fonts that are similar. Try the next few steps to learn how to find similar fonts.

5 **Click the View menu.**

The View menu sets different views and details for fonts.

Lesson 8: Working with Fonts 23

Figure 1.18
Use the Fonts folder in Control Panel to view a font before using so you can select the best font to use in a document.

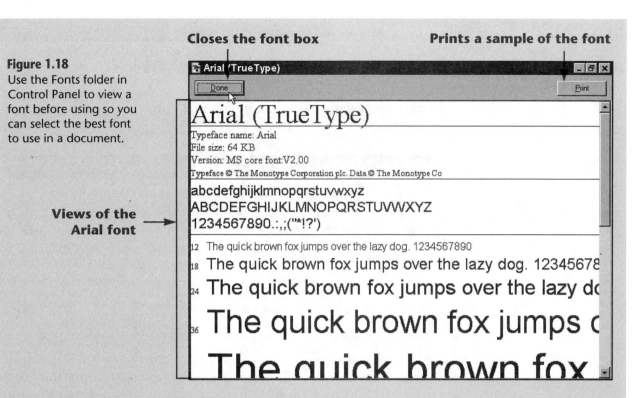

Closes the font box — Prints a sample of the font

Views of the Arial font

6 Select List Fonts by Similarity.

Your window should rearrange and Arial should be listed in the List Fonts by Similarity To box, as shown in Figure 1.19. If it is not listed, select Arial from the list by clicking the arrow to the right of the box. The font names are listed in the left column and should default to Arial because we had selected it earlier in this lesson. Their level of similarity is listed in the right column. You can also change to Similar view by clicking the Similar View button.

Figure 1.19
You can see a list of similar fonts by using the List Fonts By Similarity To option in the Fonts dialog box.

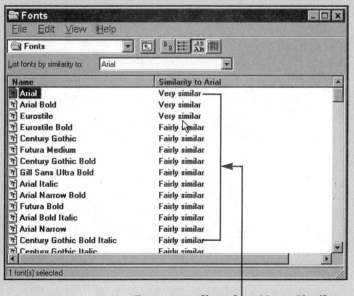

Fonts are listed as Very Similar, Fairly Similar, or Not Similar

continues

24 Project 1 Personalizing Windows 95

To Work with Fonts (continued)

7 Look at the column head of the right column.

Fonts showing a similarity to Arial, or the font you chose, will be listed in order of similarity, ranging from Very Similar to Not Similar.

If you have problems...

Some fonts have no mapping information stored with the font to describe its characteristics. If no information is available for a font, it appears at the bottom of the list and shows as Not Similar. This might mean the information is not available, rather than that it is not similar to the font you have currently chosen.

8 Press Alt+F4 to close the Fonts folder.

You can also select the File menu and choose Close.

Many people wish they could set their display fonts. Some need larger fonts so they will strain their eyes less when using the computer. In Windows 95, you can make display fonts larger or smaller. Try changing the font size used on your desktop now.

9 Right-click any blank space on your desktop and select Properties from the shortcut menu to view Display properties.

10 Select the Appearance tab.

Click the drop-down arrow of the Scheme list box. Scroll to select Windows Standard (large). Click Apply and double-click the Calculator icon on your desktop to view the results as shown in Figure 1.20.

The font size appears larger when you select a large desktop scheme

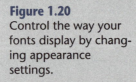
Figure 1.20
Control the way your fonts display by changing appearance settings.

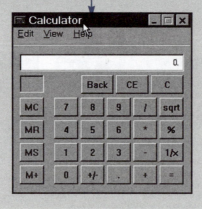

Lesson 9: Securing Your Desktop

11 **Click OK in the Display Properties dialog box to close the Calculator.**

You can return your desktop fonts to their original setting before closing the Appearance tab if you prefer.

Lesson 9: Securing Your Desktop

Windows 95 has the capability to fine tune security in corporate installations. Your systems administrator has a variety of options available when determining how to secure data in Windows 95. Corporate policy can vary widely. However, that policy will not protect you from the possibility of someone accessing your computer if it is on and you are away from your desk. After you log on to your computer or network, you share responsibility for the security of information on your computer. You can apply a password to ensure your computer is left alone when you cannot be at your computer. Try setting up a password now.

To Secure Your Desktop

1 **Right-click the desktop and choose Properties.**

The Display Properties dialog box appears.

2 **Select the Screen Saver tab.**

In addition to being able to set a screen saver in this tab, you can secure your computer from other users walking up and accessing the computer by setting a password (see Figure 1.21).

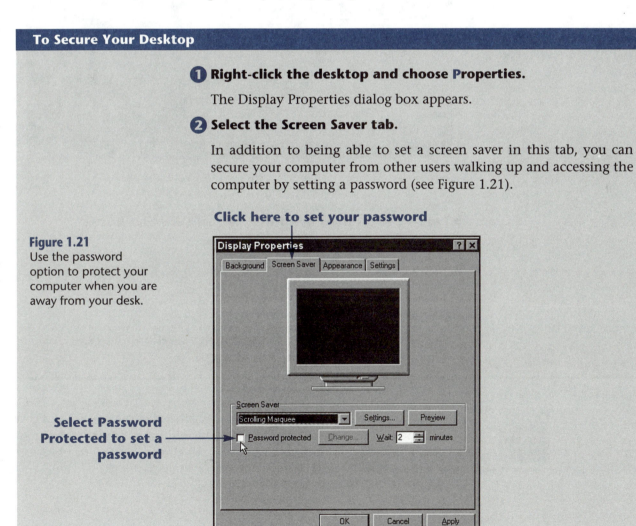

Figure 1.21
Use the password option to protect your computer when you are away from your desk.

Select Password Protected to set a password

continues

Project 1 Personalizing Windows 95

To Secure Your Desktop (continued)

❸ Select the Password Protected check box.

❹ Click the Change button.

The Change Password dialog box appears. Figure 1.22 indicates where to enter and confirm your password.

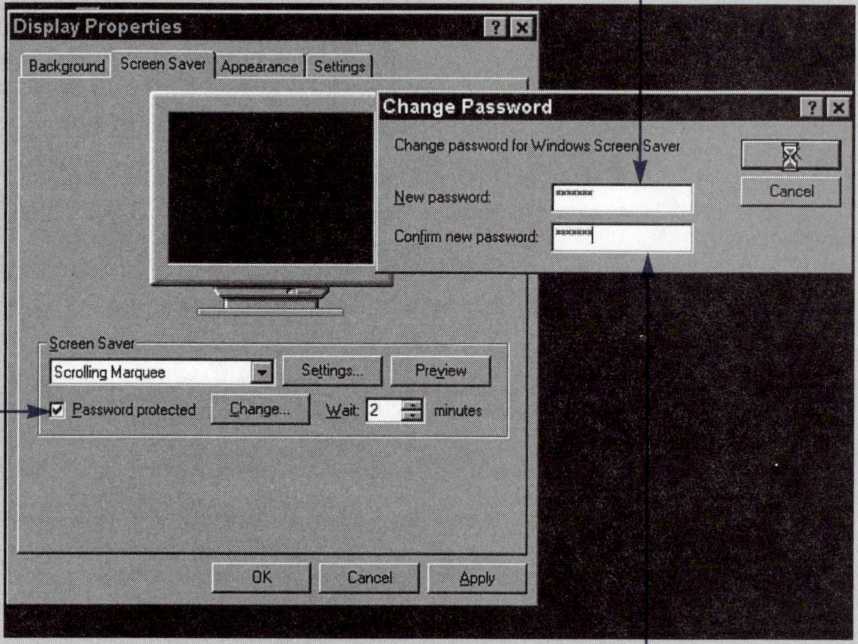

Figure 1.22
Change your password in the Change Password dialog box.

❺ Type a new password in the New Password text box.

Do not click OK.

❻ Click in the Confirm New Password text box and type the same password to confirm your request.

❼ Click OK.

❽ Click OK again to close the Display Properties dialog box. Your new password is now in effect.

To change your password, return to the Display Properties dialog box and click the Screen Saver tab. Click **C**hange. Type your old password, then the new password. Finish by confirming the password, then click OK to close the Change Password dialog box and click OK again to close the Display Properties dialog box.

Project Summary

To	Do This
Customize the Taskbar	Choose Start, **S**ettings, **T**askbar; select or deselect your choices; click **A**pply to keep the dialog box open, click OK to close the dialog box.
Put a Shortcut on Your Desktop	Right-click Start then click **E**xplore; locate the item in the Explorer; select and drag to the Start button.
Add Items to the Start Menu	Click Start, **S**ettings, **T**askbar; select the Start Menu Programs tab; click **A**dd, **Br**owse; select the file; click **O**pen, Next; select the folder to put the file in, type a name; click Finish.
Remove Items from the Start Menu	Click Start, **S**ettings, **T**askbar; select the Start Menu Programs tab; click **R**emove, Browse to select the file; click **R**emove, Close, OK.
Set How Your Program Opens	Right click Start, **O**pen; right-click the icon you want to change; choose **P**roperties; select the Shortcut tab; select Minimized or Maximized from the Run list box; click OK.
Access Recently Used Documents	Click Start, **D**ocuments, select a document.
Clear Recently Used Documents	Click Start, **S**ettings, **T**askbar, from the Start menu **C**lear, OK.
Customize My Computer	Double-click My Computer, click **V**iew, **O**ptions, adjust options on the Folder Menu tab; click OK.
View a Font	Click Start, **C**ontrol Panel; double-click the Fonts folder; double-click the font you want to see; click Done.
Find Similar Fonts	Click Start, **S**ettings, **C**ontrol Panel; select the Fonts folder; click **V**iew, select Select List Fonts by **S**imilarity, press Alt+F4 to close.
Change Display Fonts	Right-click the desktop; select **P**roperties; choose the Settings tab, click the Font Size box; select the size font you want.
Apply Security	Right-click the desktop, choose **P**roperties; select the Screen Saver tab, select the Password Protected check box; click **C**hange; type a password, confirm the password; click OK; click OK.
Move Files Using a Move to Where Box	Right-click to drag.

Project 1 Personalizing Windows 95

Select Groups on the Desktop	Click and hold down the mouse, drag to select the group.
Insert a File in a Document	Drag the file icon to the document.
Use the Run Option to Open Items	Click Start, Run; type the name or browse for the file.
Open a Shortcut Menu for an Item	Right-click the item.
Minimize All Open Windows	Right-click a blank space on the Taskbar; choose Minimize All Windows

Applying Your Skills

Customize Your Taskbar Options

1. Open the Taskbar Properties dialog box.

2. Set your Taskbar so you do not view the Taskbar if an application is open full screen in your window.

Add Shortcuts to the Desktop

1. Open My Computer

2. Locate the Clipboard icon in Windows.

3. Create a desktop shortcut to the Clipboard.

Add or Remove an Item to or from the Start Menu

1. Locate the Paint program in Windows.

2. Add Paint to your Start menu.

3. Remove Wordpad from the Start menu.

4. Set Paint to open in full screen view.

Work with Fonts

1. View all fonts similar to Times New Roman.

2. Change the view in the Font screen to view Details.

3. Change the view to List Fonts by Similarity.

Using Microsoft Exchange

Objectives

In this project, you learn how to
- ➤ Access Mail through Microsoft Exchange
- ➤ Create New Folders in Microsoft Exchange
- ➤ Set Preferences in Microsoft Exchange
- ➤ Create and Send Mail Messages
- ➤ Read and Reply to Mail Messages
- ➤ Add a Name to Your Personal Address Book

30   Project 2   Using Microsoft Exchange

Why Would I Do This?

Electronic mail, or e-mail, is any mail message forwarded to a recipient over a communications device, such as Microsoft Exchange. An e-mail could take the form of a short note, or contain many documents, including graphics or sound files. This fast and convenient form of communication saves time and money over conventional methods of mail delivery, such as Federal Express or the Post Office.

You can receive, send, and manage electronic mail (e-mail) from your desktop with Microsoft Exchange, the central messaging area in Windows 95. If your computer has a modem, you can be in touch with your office, family, associates around the world, and online services with the network capabilities built into Windows 95. Mail can contain text, graphics, and sound files. You can maintain addresses and pertinent information about the people you most frequently correspond with in Microsoft Exchange's Personal Address Book.

You need to become familiar with Microsoft Exchange features that help you communicate more effectively and with greater ease. In this project, you learn how to access Microsoft Exchange, send and receive e-mail, organize and forward mail, and manage your environment.

Lesson 1: Accessing Mail through Microsoft Exchange

Microsoft Exchange is a location in Windows 95 where you can send, receive, and manage various forms of communication such as e-mail and faxes.

For this project, Microsoft Exchange should be installed and configured in your corporate environment, and the Inbox should be visible and clearly labeled on your desktop. If the Inbox icon is not on your desktop, contact your Systems Administrator. The first thing you need to know is how to access Microsoft Exchange, so that you can become familiar with the interface.

To Access Mail through Microsoft Exchange

1 **Double-click the Inbox icon on your desktop. Microsoft Exchange opens, and your screen should look similar to Figure 2.1.**

You can also open Microsoft Exchange by choosing Start, **P**rograms, Microsoft Exchange. Either method will activate Microsoft Exchange and provide your work area, similar to a post office, but with some advantages.

Table 2.1 lists the toolbar icons Microsoft Exchange and briefly details their function. If an icon has been selected, it appears lighter on the toolbar than other items. Each icon's purpose also appears in a tool tip, which becomes visible when you pause over the icon without clicking.

Lesson 1: Accessing Mail through Microsoft Exchange 31

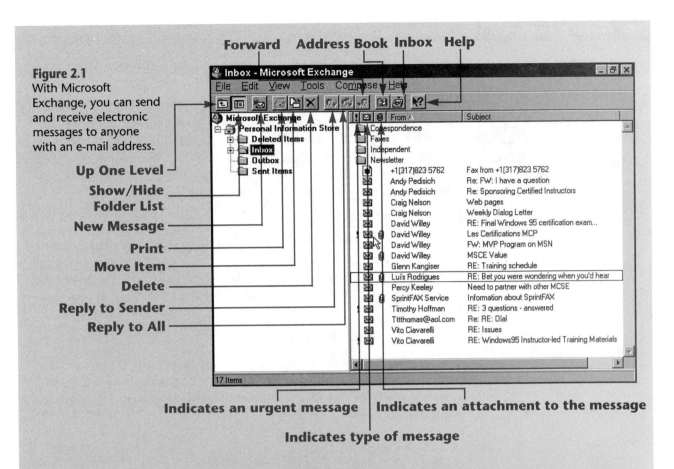

Figure 2.1
With Microsoft Exchange, you can send and receive electronic messages to anyone with an e-mail address.

If you have problems...

If your toolbar is not visible, make it visible by choosing **V**iew, **T**oolbar. A check mark appears next to the word, and the toolbar appears on the screen.

② Click the Inbox folder in the left panel of Microsoft Exchange.

Personal Information Store is the central location in Microsoft Exchange where correspondence and attached files are held.

The Inbox, Outbox, Sent Items, and Deleted Items folders are all contained in the Personal Information Store. These folders have been pre-set for you so that you can separate these types of mail, but you can add more folders to help you further coordinate items in your Personal Information Store. You can use the Personal Information Store to send, receive, share, and organize e-mail, faxes, and items from online services.

③ Click the Sent Items folder.

The Sent Items folder stores mail messages you send; it only does that if you customize Microsoft Exchange to save your sent items. See the following "Inside Stuff" for details on how to set up your Sent Items folder to store your e-mail. This can be as important as a file cabinet. If you ever need to resend an item, it will be available

continues

To Access Mail through Microsoft Exchange (continued)

for you in the Sent Items folder—eliminating the need to reconstruct the message. Of course, you need to maintain this folder to eliminate items you no longer need.

You can set preferences for how your Personal Information Store handles your mail. In Microsoft Exchange, choose **T**ools. Select **O**ptions, then click the Send tab. Select the Save a **C**opy of the Item in the "Sent Items" Folder check box (see Fig. 2.2). You can also request a receipt when a message you send is delivered or read.

4 Click the Outbox folder.

Outgoing messages you create offline are stored in the Outbox until you are ready to log on and send them. It is a good practice to create and respond to messages without being logged on to your online service, then log on and forward all completed messages at one time to save fees.

5 Click the Deleted Items folder.

The Deleted Items folder builds up quickly, especially if you set your options to notify you upon delivery of the e-mail or when the e-mail is read. You can set the Deleted Items properties to delete its contents when you log off.

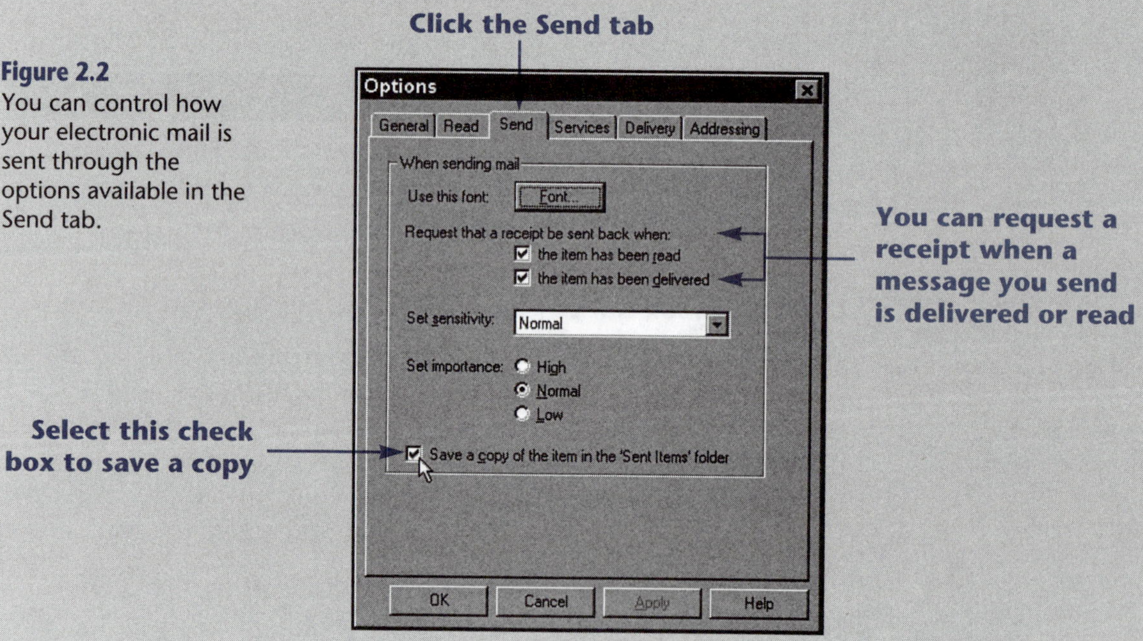

Figure 2.2
You can control how your electronic mail is sent through the options available in the Send tab.

Click the Send tab

You can request a receipt when a message you send is delivered or read

Select this check box to save a copy

Lesson 2: Creating New Folders in Microsoft Exchange

Table 2.1	Microsoft Exchange Toolbar Buttons
Button	Description
Up One Level	Moves your selection up one folder level.
Show/Hide Folder List	Click to show the folders in the area you are currently in. Click again to hide everything but the left panel contents.
New Messages	Click for fast access to a new blank e-mail message form.
Print	Prints the e-mail message.
Move Item	Moves items between folders.
Delete	Delete a mail message.
Reply to Sender	Click when you want to begin to type a reply to an e-mail you received.
Reply to All	If an e-mail is addressed to several people, you can save time by replying to everyone at once.
Forward	If you receive an e-mail and want to forward it to another person, click this button to initiate a new e-mail with the current message in the body of the e-mail.
Address Book	This is your Personal Address Book. As you receive e-mail from individuals, save the addresses in your personal address book. You can keep a variety of details regarding each entry.
Inbox	Incoming e-mail from most message providers and faxes will be stored here until you want to read them.
Help	Gets Help with Microsoft Exchange. If you click once on this button, then click any item on the screen, help will pop up with assistance and troubleshooting about the item you clicked.

Lesson 2: Creating New Folders in Microsoft Exchange

Microsoft Exchange has an interface similar to the Explorer. Like the Explorer, you can create new folders to organize your e-mail. You'll be surprised at how quickly your Inbox items accrue. You will often have to keep an e-mail for its information rather than delete it. Imagine how hard it would be to find an e-mail from a month ago without an organization system.

Avoid confusion and organize your folders now so that you will be able to find a specific item if you need it. Consider a file-management method that works for you, and apply that system from the first day you use your e-mail feature. This lesson explains how to create folders so that you can group items by your criteria and easily find an item if you need it. Folders are not, however, created in the same way they are created in the Explorer. Follow the steps below to create a folder in your Inbox.

To Create a New Folder in Microsoft Exchange

1 Click once on the Inbox in the left panel of Microsoft Exchange.

This informs Exchange that you will be working in the Inbox area. It allows you to view the current contents of the Inbox. You should see headers for any e-mail that currently reside in the Inbox. The Inbox also can contain folders, which you can create to store related e-mail.

2 Choose File, New Folder.

Notice that New Folder has an ellipsis (...) after it. This tells you that the option needs further information from you. You can use this option to create a new folder, which is the equivalent of a subdirectory in earlier versions of Windows. The New Folder dialog box appears, as shown in Figure 2.3.

Figure 2.3
Use folders to organize messages by topic, sender, or any other criteria.

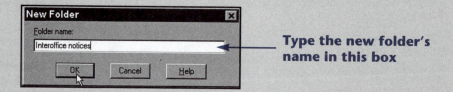

3 Type Interoffice notices in the Folder Name text box.

Remember, you do not need to limit the number of characters in your title. This helps you organize and locate folders and files in the method most suitable for your needs.

4 Click OK.

The name is accepted. The new folder is inserted into the Inbox. The new folder icon and name appear in the right panel of the Exchange window. You can use this same procedure to create new folders in Outbox, Sent Items, or Deleted Items.

5 Click the Outbox folder.

You might want to send groups of similar messages at one time. If you have responsibility for receiving and approving invoices, you

Lesson 3: Setting Preferences in Microsoft Exchange 35

can create a folder in your Outbox to hold new invoices until you can verify and approve them. Then, as you approve them, you can forward them.

6 Choose File, New Folder.

The New Folder dialog box appears (refer to Figure 2.3).

7 In the Folder Name text box, type Invoices to Verify.

The Invoices to Verify folder appears in the right panel of Exchange. As invoices come in, you can move them to this folder so that you have a central location for all invoices received.

You can expand, contract, move, and delete folders and files in Microsoft Exchange just as you can in the Explorer or My Computer.

Lesson 3: Setting Preferences in Microsoft Exchange

In addition to the obvious screen elements exclusive to Microsoft Exchange, several options appear on the menus but are not readily visible. These options allow you to further refine your working area to your requirements. In Lesson 3, you set Microsoft Exchange to warn you before an item is deleted, set the importance level of delivered mail, to verify mail delivery, and other ways to control how Microsoft Exchange handles your mail. Because you are new to Microsoft Exchange, the first thing to set is that you are warned before any item is actually deleted. The next few steps help you protect from accidental loss.

To Set Preferences in Microsoft Exchange

1 Choose Tools, Options.

This opens the Options dialog box, which provides a number of ways to control how you view and send your messages. The Tools menu is feature-rich, providing access to your Personal Address Book. The Find option lets you search for mail files based on certain criteria. Microsoft Mail Tools allows you to download address lists from services such as Microsoft Network (MSN), schedule remote mail delivery, or view your session log.

2 Click the General tab.

You should default to the General tab, but if you default to another tab, click to select it. Figure 2.4 shows the options on the General tab.

continues

To Set Preferences in Microsoft Exchange (continued)

Figure 2.4
Use this dialog box to personalize Microsoft Exchange.

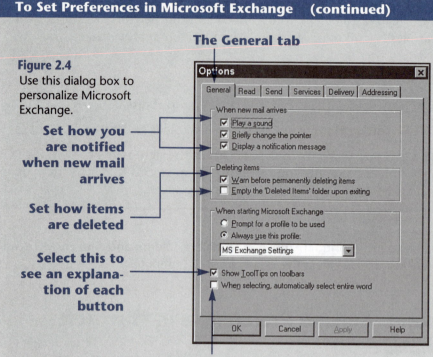

Set how you are notified when new mail arrives

Set how items are deleted

Select this to see an explanation of each button

The General tab

Choose how to select your text

❸ Go to the Deleting Items area of the General tab, and confirm that the Warn Before Permanently Deleting Items check box has a check mark in it.

The option is selected if there is a check mark in the check box. It is a good idea to provide this protection against accidentally deleting messages while you are still becoming familiar with Exchange. Next, you'll change how you receive your notification of messages. These options are located in the When New Mail Arrives section.

❹ Select the Briefly Change the Pointer check box.

Now, when you check for new mail delivery, your cursor will change to a cursor with a small envelope attached when you have new mail to read. You could also set options to play a sound or display a message when new mail is being delivered to your Inbox.

❺ Click the Read tab (see Fig. 2.5).

In this tab, you control how your mail is presented to you, and how responses you send will look to others.

Lesson 3: Setting Preferences in Microsoft Exchange 37

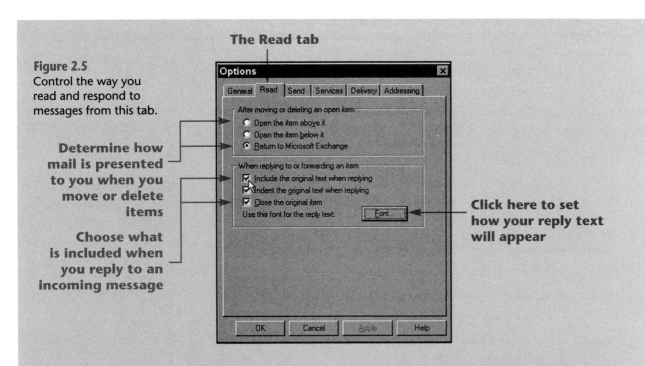

Figure 2.5
Control the way you read and respond to messages from this tab.

— The Read tab
— Determine how mail is presented to you when you move or delete items
— Choose what is included when you reply to an incoming message
— Click here to set how your reply text will appear

❻ Select Include the Original Text When Replying check box.

If the option is already selected, do not deselect the box. Selecting this option tells Microsoft Exchange to include the original message below your response when you respond to an incoming message. Notice the Font button to the right of this area. You can control the font and font color used when replying to messages if you do not want to keep the current defaults.

❼ Select the Send tab (see Figure 2.6).

Here, you control how items you create are sent. This includes the font used, the level of urgency, and whether you want a receipt when the item is delivered or read. You learned how to save each item you sent in the earlier Inside Stuff. Now, you can set the system to notify you when an item is delivered and when a delivered item is read by the recipient.

continues

Project 2 Using Microsoft Exchange

To Set Preferences in Microsoft Exchange (continued)

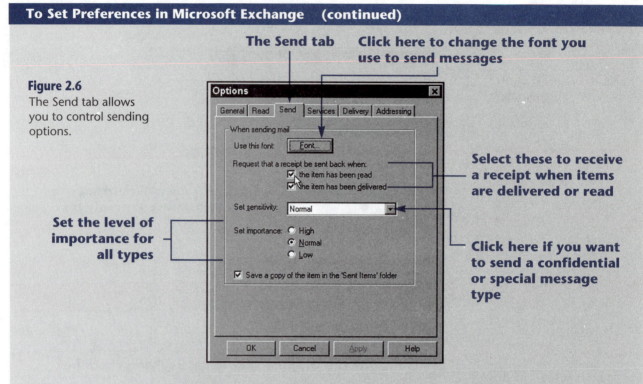

Figure 2.6
The Send tab allows you to control sending options.

8 **Select both check boxes in the Request That a Receipt Be Sent Back When section.**

The boxes next to The Item Has Been Read and The Item Has Been Delivered should now be checked.

9 **Set the importance level to Normal.**

You can set the font used for any message you originate by clicking the **F**ont button. There are three other tabs located in this Options dialog box. It is very likely that these tabs are not available for you to change items. Check with your instructor or Systems Administrator prior to changing any options available on these tabs.

10 **Click OK.**

Your new settings take effect immediately. If you want to see changes take effect while keeping the Options dialog box open, just click **A**pply instead of OK. This allows you to make changes without exiting the Options dialog box.

Table 2.2 describes each of the tabs in the Options dialog box and the options you can control through these tabs.

Lesson 4:   Creating and Sending Mail Messages   39

Table 2.2	Options Dialog Box Options
Tab	Options Available to Select
General	Set how you want to be informed when new mail arrives.
	Choose how items located in the Deleted Items folder are handled.
	Select which mailbox profile should be used. You must have a profile before using Microsoft Exchange to receive mail. Your profile might have been set by your Systems Administrator.
	Set if you want to show or hide ToolTips. (ToolTips appear when you pause over a button and explain the button.)
	Set if you automatically select an entire word when selecting text, or individual letters.
Read	Set how items appear when you read them.
	Choose how your responses are sent; what font, if the original e-mail is attached for reference, and other items.
Send	Set what your font will look like, select delivery options, and set sensitivity and importance levels. You can also choose whether you want to save a copy in your Sent Items folder.
Services	Used by Systems Administrators to set up the services available to you. In most cases, you should not change settings in this tab.
Delivery	Set where mail is to be delivered to and how recipients are processed. In most cases, you should not change settings in this tab.
Addressing	Set what address lists you use, where you keep addresses, and which address list the system should check in to confirm recipient names. In most cases, you should not change settings in this tab.

Lesson 4: Creating and Sending Mail Messages

Mail messages will quickly become an important part of your daily routine. When you communicate with others both inside and outside the office via e-mail, you will find it a necessary tool. You no longer just communicate with interoffice personnel, you can send messages to family members, friends, or any other individual who uses an e-mail service. Your instructor will inform you if there are any corporate restrictions on sending e-mail to outside people. In the following steps, you learn to create a message and send that message to another recipient.

Project 2 Using Microsoft Exchange

To Create and Send a Message

1 Click Compose.

The Compose drop-down menu is the location from which your e-mail messages and faxes are created and forwarded. You can press Ctrl+N if you prefer.

2 Choose New Message.

A blank New Message window appears. The insertion point defaults to the To text box, so that you can address the e-mail. Table 2.3 describes each of the toolbar buttons and their purposes.

You can click the New Message icon on the Inbox toolbar to initiate a new mail message instead of choosing Compose, New Message.

3 Click the To button.

You can also type in your instructor's e-mail name, but for this exercise, you will select it from the Address Book. The Address Book appears, and you can choose a name (see Figure 2.7). Corporate networking provides a seemingly limitless set of configurations available for mail environments these days. For this reason, some features of your Address Book might differ slightly from items listed here.

Use Figure 2.7 with Table 2.3 as a reference as you create your first e-mail message.

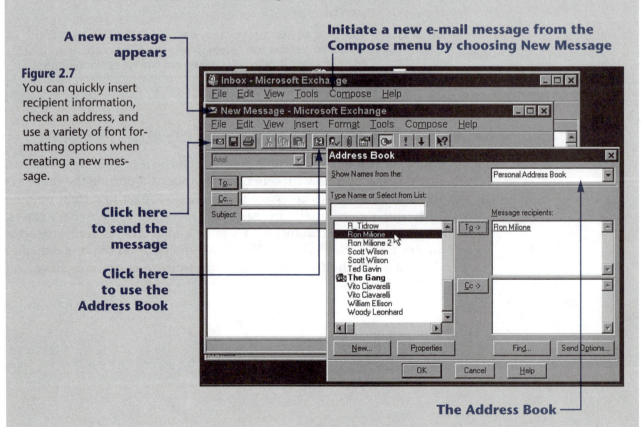

Figure 2.7
You can quickly insert recipient information, check an address, and use a variety of font formatting options when creating a new message.

A new message appears

Initiate a new e-mail message from the Compose menu by choosing New Message

Click here to send the message

Click here to use the Address Book

The Address Book

Lesson 4: Creating and Sending Mail Messages

④ Select your instructor's name from the list.

Click the To box to insert the name in the Message Recipients list. If your system is set up differently, your instructor will guide you on what steps to take to address your e-mail.

⑤ Click OK to close the Address Book.

You return to the new message you are currently creating.

⑥ Press [Tab] twice to reach the Subject text box.

Use this text box as you would the subject line of a memo.

⑦ Type Test Message.

This clearly indicates that the subject of the message (which is used as the message's mail header) is your Test Message.

⑧ Press [Tab] once.

This leaves your cursor in the body of the message. You can place text, files, and graphics in the body for transfer to recipients.

⑨ Type This is a test message (see Fig. 2.8).

When you are working in Exchange, you might find that you need to save a file you are sending to a different location on your disk (perhaps with a particular group of documents on a different computer). If you want, you can click the Save button to save a message to a specific file location.

It is more efficient to keep messages in Microsoft Exchange, under most circumstances. However, you might be sending an important file you want to save. In that case, save the message as a file in the appropriate location.

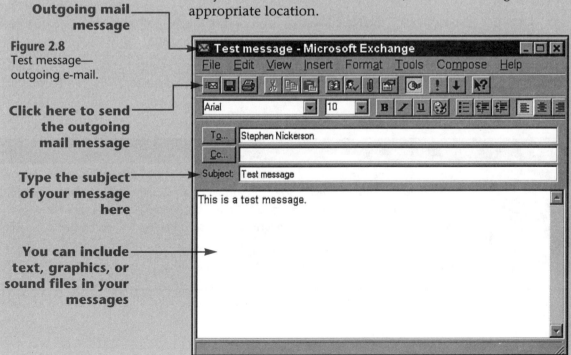

Figure 2.8 Test message—outgoing e-mail.

- Outgoing mail message
- Click here to send the outgoing mail message
- Type the subject of your message here
- You can include text, graphics, or sound files in your messages

continues

To Create and Send a Message (continued)

10 **Click the Send button to send the message.**

You can set your options to inform you when an item is delivered to the recipient. You can also set your preferences to show when the e-mail was accessed and read by the recipient. This is a very useful tool for important messages. Refer to Lesson 3 if you have any questions about this topic.

If you have problems...

Because your e-mail was ready to use in your corporate environment, you should not have any problems when addressing to your instructor. If, however, you do run into trouble when addressing e-mail, you can click the Check Names button on the toolbar or choose **T**ools, Chec**k** Names.

Make sure you are checking names in the appropriate locations. For example, if you are sending to your secretary, and she is in your personal Address Book, you might use this as your area from which to check names. If you do not have the individual whose name you are checking listed in your personal Address Book, change this option to Microsoft Network or the preferred carrier for your system.

After you do this, you can search for the name by either typing the name in the Type Name In text box, selecting the name from the list, or using the Find button to search the available listing of similar names. Choose the name carefully to avoid sending the e-mail to the wrong individual.

You can click the New Message icon on the Inbox toolbar to initiate a new mail message instead of choosing Co**m**pose, **N**ew Message.

You can easily address your e-mail to multiple recipients. To do this, place a semicolon after each name, then type the next addressee. You can handle cc's the same way.

Jargon Watch

A **cc** is a term held over from days that were less technologically oriented—cc literally stands for carbon copy. A piece of carbon paper would be placed between two sheets of typing paper, then inserted into the typewriter. As the typewriter keys pounded on the paper, the carbon imprinted a second copy of the document.

However, today a cc means a copy of the original document meant to be sent to an individual other than the recipient.

Lesson 4: Creating and Sending Mail Messages   43

Table 2.3   Microsoft E-Mail Elements

Element	Description
Send	When you finish typing your message, whether online or off, click this button to send your message.
	If you are offline, Exchange moves the message to your Outbox and the message will be forwarded the next time you log on to the Microsoft Network.
Save	Saves e-mail.
Print	Prints e-mail.
Cut	You can manipulate text in your e-mail with a familiar interface similar in features to Word for Windows.
	Use Cut as you would in any Windows application. You can also press Ctrl+X to cut selected text.
Copy	Copies text. You can also press Ctrl+C to copy selected text.
Paste	Pastes text. You can also press Ctrl+V to paste selected text.
	You can also use drag-and-drop features if you prefer.
Address Book	This is your personal address book, unless your options have been set to another resource.
	You can check this by clicking Tools, Options and looking at the Addressing tab. The Show This List First text box states what service has been selected as the default choice.
Check Names	You might receive a message informing you that the individual you have addressed your message to does not exist. Use Check Names to find and verify the correct access name for that individual.
Insert File	Equivalent to choosing Insert, File.
Properties	Displays the properties of the message, such as its priority level and delivery verification options.
Read Receipt	Requests or cancels your request to be informed when a message has been read.
Importance High	Marks a message as an urgent message.
Importance Low	Sends a message as low priority.
Help	Features help exclusively for mailing. Click once, then click the item you want to find out information about, and the Help window will appear with help located to that topic.

Lesson 5: Reading and Replying to Mail Messages

Windows 95 provides a number of ways to retrieve new mail messages, depending on your preference. You can have your mail automatically downloaded when you open your mail system, which could be set through a variety of accesses, such as Microsoft Mail or Microsoft Network. You can retrieve messages when you want, or you can check headers (subjects, sender names, and other pertinent identifying information) before deciding what mail to accept. In this lesson, you learn the most popular retrieval method offered in Microsoft Exchange.

To Retrieve New Mail Messages

1 **Click the Inbox in the left panel of Microsoft Exchange.**

This allows you to view the current contents of the Inbox.

2 **Click Tools, Deliver Now Using.**

The submenu appears (see Fig. 2.9). You can receive your mail from many resources. Your instructor will advise you which service to select when retrieving mail on your corporate system. Note that the term "Deliver" is used by Microsoft to receive mail in this circumstance. If you subscribe to many services, you might choose to receive mail from all services simultaneously. You do not have to be logged on at this time.

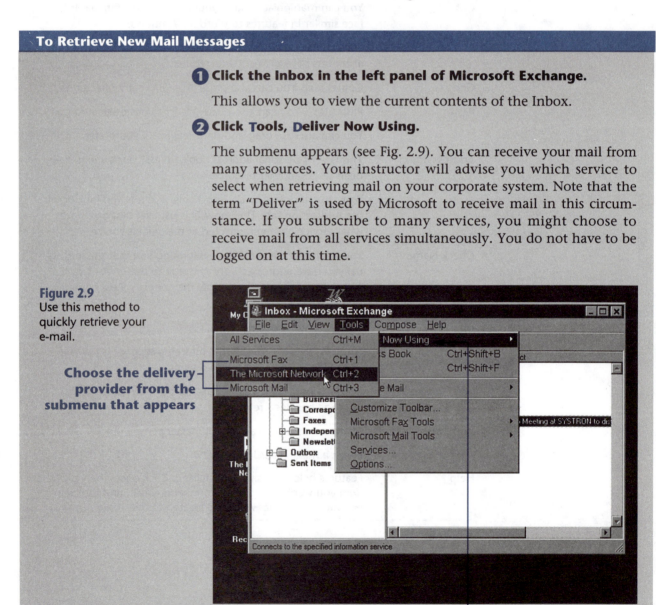

Figure 2.9
Use this method to quickly retrieve your e-mail.

Choose the delivery provider from the submenu that appears

Choose Tools, Deliver Now Using

Lesson 5: Reading and Replying to Mail Messages

❸ Choose the service provided by your instructor and release your mouse button.

If you are already logged on to the service, the search begins immediately. If you are not currently logged on, the logon screen appears, so that you can receive incoming messages. This example uses Microsoft Network, but your service might differ.

❹ Type your User ID and password, and click Connect.

Microsoft Network will log on and automatically carry out the command to search for and deliver messages to your Inbox. New messages appear in bold print. Microsoft Network disconnects after retrieving messages, unless you accessed e-mail while already connected the Microsoft Network. You should see an e-mail message from your instructor in your messages received.

❺ Double-click your mail message header to open and read it (see Fig. 2.10).

You can reply directly in your e-mail screen. There are three ways you can reply to a message:

➤ *Reply to Sender*. If you click this button, your reply will be sent directly to only the individual who originally sent it to you.

➤ *Reply to All*. If you click this button, your reply will be sent to everyone on the list of addressees.

➤ *Forward*. You can forward a copy of the e-mail you received to anyone you want. Click the Forward button. When the forward screen pops up, type the name of the individual you want to forward the e-mail to in the **To** box or select the name from the Address Book.

Figure 2.10
Double-click the mail message header to open an incoming message.

Click this button to reply to the sender

Original incoming e-mail

continues

To Retrieve New Mail Messages (continued)

6 **Choose the Reply to Sender button now.**

The Reply window appears. The cursor appears in the response area.

7 **Type your message in the response area (see Fig. 2.11).**

Type this message: **Thank you for the kind offer!** Click the Send icon to send the message.

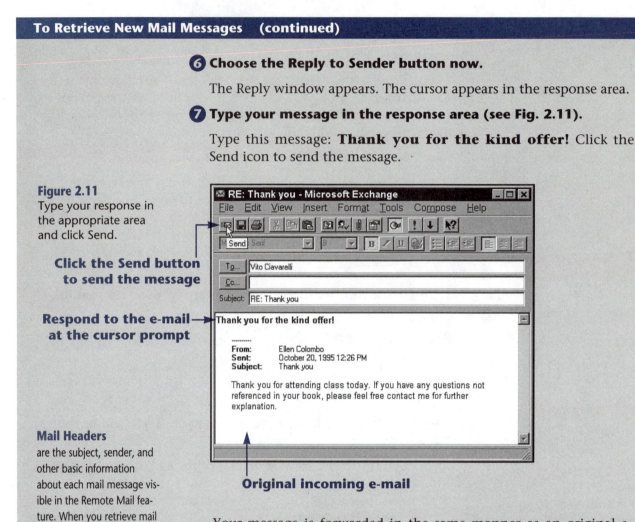

Figure 2.11
Type your response in the appropriate area and click Send.

Click the Send button to send the message

Respond to the e-mail at the cursor prompt

Original incoming e-mail

Mail Headers are the subject, sender, and other basic information about each mail message visible in the Remote Mail feature. When you retrieve mail headers, you will see the subject, sender, and other basic information about each mail message. You can then copy messages from the server, move them directly to your Inbox, or delete them without reading.

Your message is forwarded in the same manner as an original e-mail is forwarded. While this is the most popular method of mail delivery, there are other methods. Remote Mail delivery allows you to further manipulate mail receipt. With Remote Mail delivery, you can view mail headers while your mail remains on the server. Then download only those items you want to retrieve. You can also send outgoing mail that you created offline. If you think this method might fit your situation, ask your instructor to advise you on this.

Lesson 6: Adding a Name to Your Personal Address Book

Although e-mail is extremely popular, it is still a relatively new technology and requires some getting used to. Such technologies as e-mail and online services will most likely bring new friends and associates from around the world into your personal and professional life. You will be amazed at how quickly your e-mail Inbox fills. Use the steps below to learn some ways to add an e-mail contact to your Personal Address Book.

Lesson 6: Adding a Name to Your Personal Address Book 47

To Add a Name to Your Personal Address Book

1 In Microsoft Exchange, choose **T**ools, **A**ddress Book (see Fig. 2.12).

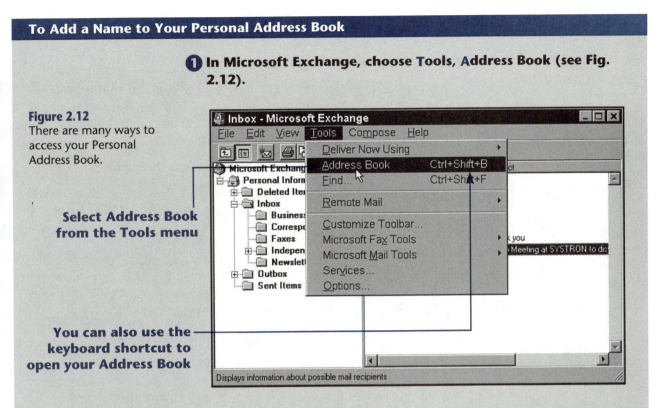

Figure 2.12
There are many ways to access your Personal Address Book.

Select Address Book from the Tools menu

You can also use the keyboard shortcut to open your Address Book

Notice a shortcut to your Personal Address Book is provided on the **T**ools menu. You can use the keyboard shortcut instead of the menu by pressing Ctrl+Shift+B. You can also click the Address Book button to activate the Personal Address Book. The Address Book appears (see Fig. 2.13).

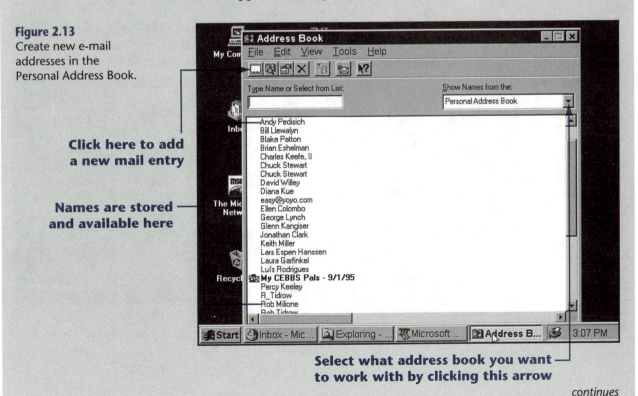

Figure 2.13
Create new e-mail addresses in the Personal Address Book.

Click here to add a new mail entry

Names are stored and available here

Select what address book you want to work with by clicking this arrow

continues

48 Project 2 Using Microsoft Exchange

To Add a Name to Your Personal Address Book (continued)

② Choose File, New Entry.

The New Entry dialog box appears. Each service currently available to you is listed in this dialog box. Ask your instructor which service to select from for this example. You will be adding the name of your instructor to your Personal Address Book.

③ Select the service per your instructors' instructions.

The default location for this entry is your Personal Address Book, but notice that you have the option to change the location.

④ Click OK.

The New Entry dialog box closes. In this example, the Microsoft Network is the service used. If your service is different from MSN, your screen may vary from this example. The New The Microsoft Network Member Properties dialog box appears (see Figure 2.14).

⑤ Enter the member ID and name of your instructor.

Your instructor will guide you if any information differs from Figure 2.14. You also have tabs to add phone numbers, pager numbers, fax numbers, professional notes, and other information pertinent to this listing.

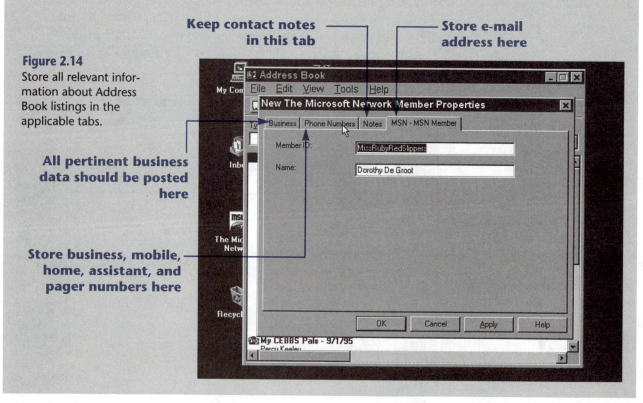

Figure 2.14
Store all relevant information about Address Book listings in the applicable tabs.

Keep contact notes in this tab

Store e-mail address here

All pertinent business data should be posted here

Store business, mobile, home, assistant, and pager numbers here

Project Summary 49

6 Click OK.

The entry now appears in your Personal Address Book. Close the Address Book Properties box. You can choose File, Close instead of clicking OK.

7 Right-click the new entry.

A shortcut menu appears. You can view the properties of an entry or delete an entry from this menu.

8 Choose Delete.

This clears the entry from your Address Book.

9 Close your Address Book.

Close Microsoft Exchange.

If you receive an e-mail and want to post the entry to your Personal Address Book, but do not have the senders' information, you can place your cursor directly over the individuals' name in the e-mail, right-click, and select Add to Personal Address Book.

Project Summary

To	Do This
Access mail	Double-click the Inbox.
Move around in mail	Click the item.
Create a new folder	Choose File, New Folder; type the new folder name, click OK.
Set preferences	Choose Tools, Options, select the tab and option, click OK.
Read messages	Choose Tools, Deliver Now Using, select the provider (connect to the provider), double-click the message.
Reply to messages	Click Reply to Sender, type the message, click the Send icon.
Retrieve mail messages remotely	Choose Tools, Remote Mail, The Microsoft Network; click the Mark to Retrieve button; choose Tools, Connect and Transfer Mail, OK; logon; view headers, mark messages; choose Connect and Transfer Mail, OK, Tools, Disconnect.
Create a new mail message	Choose Compose, New Message; address and type the message, click the Send button.

continues

50 Project 2 Using Microsoft Exchange

To	Do This
Expand mail tree	Press the plus (+) key on the folder you want to explain.
Collapse the tree	Press the minus (–) key.
Move folders	Drag to the new location.
Copy folders or messages	Press Ctrl while you drag the folder or message.
Change displayed columns	Choose File, Open, View, Columns, add columns you want, click Add, OK.

Applying Your Skills

Create a New Folder

1. Select the Inbox.

2. Create a new folder in the Inbox named Business.

3. Create a new folder in the Inbox named Personal.

Setting Preferences in Microsoft Exchange

1. Change your mail delivery to notify you with a sound when mail is delivered.

2. Select Arial as the font to be used for outgoing e-mail.

3. Set your response options to indent the senders' original message.

4. Deselect the option that saves sent items in the Sent Items folder.

Sending E-Mail

1. Open a new e-mail form.

2. Send an e-mail to your instructor stating a question you have from the current class.

3. Forward your e-mail.

Personal Address Book

1. Open the Personal Address Book.

2. Select your instructors' name.

3. Use the shortcut menu to delete the current listing.

Project

3

Printing, Modems, and Faxing

Objectives

In this project, you learn how to

➤ Set Up a Printer

➤ Set Up a Modem

➤ Use HyperTerminal with Your Modem to Connect to a Remote Computer

➤ Set Up Your Fax Settings

➤ Send a Fax Using Fax Wizard

➤ Receive Faxes

➤ Work with Dial-Up Networking

➤ Use Phone Dialer

52 Project 3 Printing, Modems, and Faxing

Why Would I Do This?

n this project, you learn ways to maximize your efficiency with the power of peripheral support built into Windows 95. Much of the power of the PC is not in the PC itself, but in the **peripherals** that are attached to it, such as the printer, modem, and fax. Peripherals allow us to take our work beyond the PC and share it with the outside world in a number of ways.

With Windows 95, you can send a document to print, even if you don't have a printer currently attached. Windows will remember your request and print your document as soon as you reattach your computer to a printer. If your computer has a modem and Windows 95, you can connect to the world via e-mail, fax, the Internet, and the World Wide Web to access information.

It is possible to send and receive faxes directly from your computer with Windows 95. First, you need to learn how to set up the printer and modem so you can receive and print items. Then, you learn how to dial other computers to access information from resources other than your computer, and interact with others who work with a modem.

Lesson 1: Setting Up a Printer

In the past, it has been difficult to set up a printer, even in an environment as friendly as Windows 3.11. You needed to know port settings and configuration information. Windows 95 does all that for you and provides wizards to guide you through the setup process. You are asked only basic questions; Windows 95 sets up the hardware for you, basing its actions on your responses.

Before you take the following steps to set up your printer, remember that many printers can be connected to any server in a networked environment. Throughout this book, you will be working closely with your instructor to ensure that you are connecting to and accessing the correct peripherals, such as a printer for this lesson. Please do not start this exercise until your instructor or Systems Administrator tells you which printer to use for this lesson.

To Set Up a Printer

❶ Click the Start button.

After you become familiar with how Windows 95 approaches tasks, you can see that you can use the Start button to access anything you need on your computer.

❷ Choose Settings.

When you choose **S**ettings, you see a submenu. This submenu includes **T**askbar, which you saw in Project 1 when you fine-tuned

Lesson 1: Setting Up a Printer 53

your Start menu preferences and Taskbar options; **C**ontrol Panel, which holds most hardware settings; and **P**rinters, which controls the printer settings for all the printers your machine uses.

❸ Choose Printers.

The Printers folder opens, revealing the Printers window (see Fig. 3.1). The Printers window displays icons for each printer you use. Of course, given the wide variety of printers and printer configurations currently available, your screen will differ from Figure 3.1.

Your Printers window should open with the Add Printer option on the top line. If you prefer to use the keyboard, press the (Spacebar), then press (⏎Enter). This action is equivalent to selecting the Add printer icon with your mouse and clicking OK.

You can also open the Add Printer Wizard if you click Add Printer, then choose **F**ile, **O**pen. You can also use the shortcut menu (right-click Add Printer) to open the Add Printer Wizard.

Figure 3.1
Use the Printers window to locate available printers and access new printers to use.

Manage all printers through the Printers window

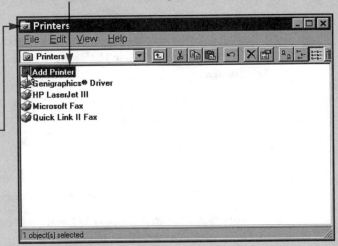

Double-click here to open the Add Printer Wizard

❹ Double-click the Add Printer icon. The Add Printer Wizard opens, as shown in Figure 3.2.

The Wizard explains each step to you, and prompts you for information when necessary. You need to know whether the printer you want to connect to is connected to your computer or to a network before moving to the next step. Most corporate computers are attached to the network.

continues

54 Project 3 Printing, Modems, and Faxing

To Set Up a Printer (continued)

Figure 3.2
You can add new printers easily with the Add Printer Wizard's step-by-step assistance.

The Add Printer Wizard walks you through the set up of your printer

❺ Click Next.

In the next screen, the Wizard asks how the new printer is connected to your computer; whether your printer is connected to your computer or to another computer on the network.

❻ Click Local Printer if you are not connected to the network. Click Network Printer if the printer is connected to a network.

Check with your Systems Administrator or instructor if you are not sure of the correct answer. Click Next to continue to the next Add Printer screen, where you can specify the printer's manufacturer and model as shown in Figure 3.3.

❼ Select the printer's manufacturer from the Manufacturers list. Select the printer model from the Printers list.

❽ If you need to install printer software with your printer, click the Have Disk button.

Some printer models require a separate installation disk. Ask your system administrator or instructor if you need to use a separate disk.

Lesson 1: Setting Up a Printer 55

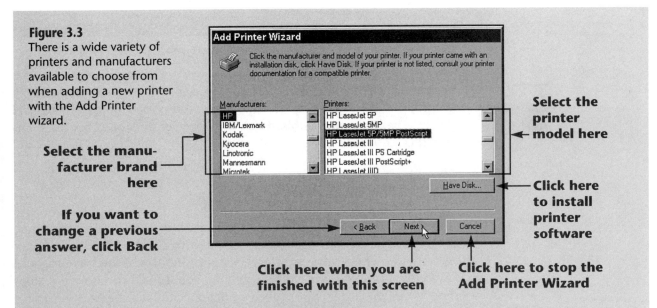

Figure 3.3
There is a wide variety of printers and manufacturers available to choose from when adding a new printer with the Add Printer wizard.

9 **Click Next.**

Windows 95 reads the computer hardware and also looks for the correct printer driver to use for the printer selected. Available Ports are displayed in this screen. Unless your Systems Administrator tells you otherwise, accept the selection in this screen.

10 **Click Next.**

In the next screen, you are prompted to give the new printer a name and set printer defaults. Verify or correct the Printer Name, and specify whether you want this to be your default printer.

11 **Click Next.**

This is the final screen of the Add Printer Wizard. You are prompted to print a test page, if you want. Select Yes to print a test page. If a test page prints successfully, you have correctly set up the printer.

12 **Click Finish to complete the Add Printer setup.**

The printer is successfully installed for use with your computer. The Add Printer Wizard closes. If you look in your Printers folder, you see the new printer available.

A message informs you that the test page is being printed, and inquires whether the page printed correctly. If your page prints correctly, click Yes. If your page does not print correctly, consult your instructor to troubleshoot the printer connection. You can close the Printers folder if your test page prints correctly.

56 Project 3 Printing, Modems, and Faxing

> **If you have problems...**
>
> Make sure you turn on your printer before you print your test page.

 If you are using a network printer or if you need to switch to another network printer, there is an easier way to connect to the printer you want to use. Double-click the Network Neighborhood icon on your desktop. Click the printer's icon, then choose **F**ile, **I**nstall.

Lesson 2: Setting Up a Modem

Windows 95's mobile features center on a modem. You use a modem to retrieve e-mail, faxes, and online services, and to connect directly to your office computer when working from a remote site. If you are traveling and your Systems Administrator is not available, you'll need to know the steps to set up a modem correctly. In this lesson, you set up a modem.

It is imperative that you coordinate closely with your instructor during this and future lessons. Given the myriad of hardware and configuration options available to a user for any lessons involving networking, printers, modems, and communications hardware, you should check with your instructor to verify the correct hardware and access options you will work with in these examples.

To Set up a Modem

Modem
A **modem** is a communications device that attaches the computer to a telephone line to facilitate communications flow between hardware. Note, however, that if your company has a direct Internet connection, you could be using a network adapter card rather than a modem.

1 Click the Start button.

2 Choose **S**ettings, **C**ontrol Panel.

There are a large number of options you can work with in the Control Panel. In this exercise, you work with the modem settings.

3 Double-click Modems.

The Modem Properties dialog box appears, as shown in Figure 3.4. This dialog box provides ways for you to add or remove a modem, and to adjust the modem properties or the dialing properties of any modem used with your system.

Lesson 2: Setting Up a Modem   57

Figure 3.4
Install new modems, and change and diagnose modem settings in the Modems Properties dialog box.

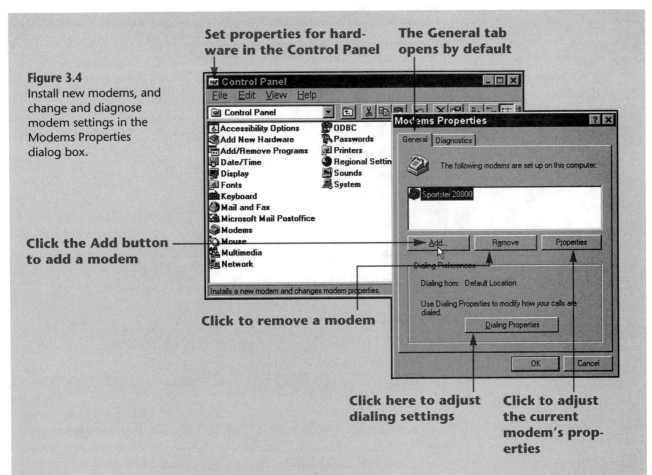

4 Click Add.

The Install New Modem Wizard appears. This wizard walks you through setting up your modem. Before you begin, make sure you are not using any programs that require a modem. You also need to make sure that the modem and computer are attached. Remember that many modems in newer computers are internal. Let the Modem Wizard detect your hardware—unless you know that it will cause problems with your model.

5 Click Next.

Windows 95 reads your system and looks for any attached modems. Then a dialog box appears, verifying the modem found connected to the computer, as shown in Figure 3.5.

continues

To Set Up a Modem (continued)

Figure 3.5
Windows 95 identifies the new modem and offers you an opportunity to change that information.

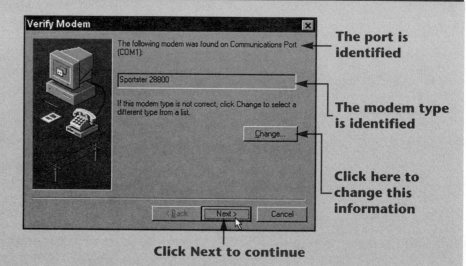

- The port is identified
- The modem type is identified
- Click here to change this information
- Click Next to continue

⑥ Click Next.

The Install Modem wizard sets up the modem and presents a screen informing you that the modem has been set up successfully.

⑦ Click Finish.

You can fine-tune modem settings in the Modems Properties dialog box. The Modems Properties dialog box should still be open when you finish the Wizard. Remember, to access the Modems Properties dialog box, double-click Modems in the Control Panel.

⑧ Click the Properties button in the Modems Properties dialog box and view the current speaker volume setting for the modem you have installed.

The speaker volume is clearly indicated on the General tab of the Modems Properties dialog box. When modems dial in to connect to a service or other communications device, they can be set to varying volumes. If it is set to a high volume, and you do not want to hear a sound, drag the Volume lever to Off.

⑨ Click OK.

This closes the Properties dialog box when adjusting the speaker volume.

⑩ Click Close to exit completely out of Modems Properties.

Lesson 3:   Using HyperTerminal to Connect to a Remote Computer   59

Lesson 3: Using HyperTerminal to Connect to a Remote Computer

The HyperTerminal feature works with your modem to provide a way for you to connect to a remote computer. When you connect to a remote computer, you can transfer files or information, even if one computer is not running Windows 95. You can also use HyperTerminal to send and receive files from e-mail standards like CompuServe or MCI Mail. If both computers use Windows 95, use Dial-Up Networking instead (discussed in Lesson 7).

In this lesson, you learn how to use HyperTerminal to connect your PC to another PC that is using a different operating system. In the first few steps, you start HyperTerminal and configure it for your use.

To Use HyperTerminal with Your Modem to Connect to a Remote Computer

1 Click Start, select Programs, Accessories, then HyperTerminal.

This opens the HyperTerminal window, as shown in Figure 3.6. You can see CompuServe and several other service provider icons. There might be additional providers listed in your HyperTerminal window, depending on what services were installed by your Systems Administrator.

The HyperTerminal window shows connection options

Figure 3.6
You can use HyperTerminal to connect to computers not using Windows 95 and to transfer files.

Double-click your selection to begin

2 Double-click the CompuServe icon.

A dialog box appears, asking you to confirm your modem because HyperTerminal has not yet been configured.

3 Click OK.

This opens a dialog box that lets you configure the service you want to connect to (see Figure 3.7). In this example, I used CompuServe

continues

Project 3 Printing, Modems, and Faxing

To Use HyperTerminal with Your Modem to Connect to a Remote Computer (continued)

because it is currently the most popular communications service. However, if CompuServe is not used for this lesson, your instructor will guide you through the lesson using a different service or computer to access.

The Phone Number dialog box allows you to change the phone number you are dialing, the access number, and the dialing properties used to make the connection.

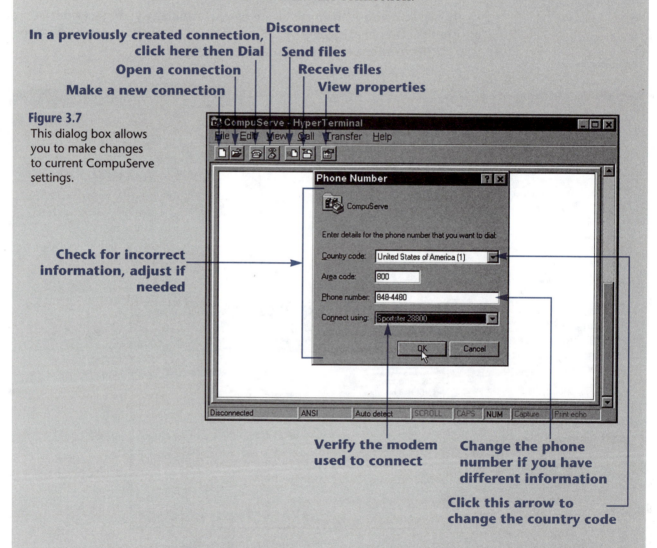

Figure 3.7
This dialog box allows you to make changes to current CompuServe settings.

④ **Modify any incorrect phone numbers or dialing properties.**

You will most likely have default numbers listed in the available boxes in the Phone Dialer dialog box. If the service you want to connect to has a new number or if you have changed modems, you need to modify this information. Your instructor will provide the correct access information to use.

Lesson 3: Using HyperTerminal to Connect to a Remote Computer   61

❺ Click OK.

The Phone Dialer dialog box closes. The system confirms your settings and gives you an opportunity to make last-minute changes in the Connect dialog box (see Figure 3.8).

❻ Click the Dial Now button to connect to CompuServe.

The Connect dialog box appears, displaying the dialing and connection process status. You connect to CompuServe. After you connect, you can work as usual in the service. If you need to view the current settings for a particular service, select the service in the HyperTerminal window, then right-click and select Properties from the shortcut menu that appears. You can also choose File, Properties or choose the Properties button on the toolbar. If you need to connect to another service, you can do so in the HyperTerminal screen.

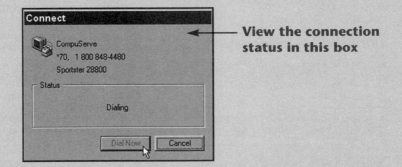

Figure 3.8
HyperTerminal displays the status of the connection you are attempting to make.

View the connection status in this box

The preceding steps in this lesson provided the information you need when you open HyperTerminal and need to make a new connection to a particular computer or service. However, after the connection is created, you most likely will find you'll need to access the same computer frequently. The steps taken to connect to a computer when the initial connection file has already been created are different from the steps you used to set up the original connection. Follow the remainder of this lesson to see how you will use HyperTerminal on a day-to-day basis. You are still in the HyperTerminal window.

❼ Choose File, Open.

Double-click to select the file you want to use. Ask your instructor which connection file to use for this example.

❽ Choose Call, Connect.

You can use the Connect button located on the toolbar, if you prefer. You might find that your system has been configured to display the Connect dialog box automatically. When the Connect dialog box appears, click Dial to dial your connection.

Project 3 Printing, Modems, and Faxing

Table 3.1 explains the features in HyperTerminal and quickly lists steps you can take to perform these functions. Use Table 3.1 to familiarize yourself with common HyperTerminal procedures.

Table 3.1 HyperTerminal Features	
Feature	Procedure
To call a remote computer	Choose File, Open; double-click the connection; choose Call, Connect; click Dial.
To send a file	Choose Transfer, Send File, type the path and file name. Click the Send button. If you need to change the protocol, select it from the Protocol drop-down list.
To receive a file from	Download the file to your computer using the remote computer software; choose Transfer, Receive File; type the path in which to store the file; click the remote computer protocol in the Use Receiving Protocol drop-down list, click the Receive button.
To adjust window size	Choose View, Font; select a larger point size to enlarge the window; a smaller point size to shrink the window; click OK; right-click in the terminal screen and select Snap.
To get help	Select Help, Help Topics in HyperTerminal for specific HyperTerminal and modem troubleshooting assistance.

Lesson 4: Setting Up Your Fax

With the Windows 95 operating system and a modem, you have the equivalent of a complete fax machine available at any time in your own computer. You harness this service through the Microsoft Exchange client, which organizes your e-mail, faxes, and all other remote message services.

Faxes are received electronically, similar to e-mail. You can print or edit a fax you receive. Faxing and file transfer is as easy as printing a document in Windows 95. Now that you have your own fax machine, you need to set your preferences and options to suit your requirements. In this lesson, you customize this information in Microsoft Exchange.

To Set Up Your Fax

❶ Double-click the Inbox icon on your desktop.

This activates your Inbox, located in Microsoft Exchange. Microsoft Exchange holds all your e-mail messages and faxes.

❷ Choose Tools, Microsoft Fax Tools, then choose Options from the submenu (see Figure 3.9).

Lesson 4: Setting Up Your Fax

The Microsoft Fax Properties dialog box opens, as shown in Figure 3.10.

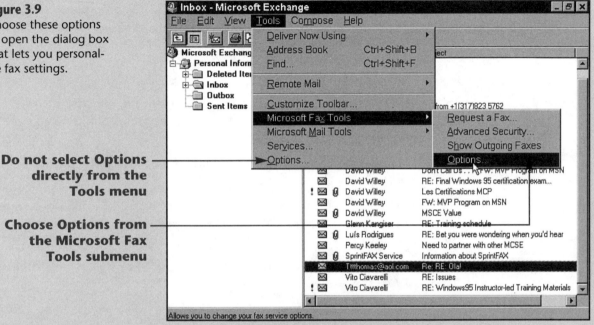

Figure 3.9
Choose these options to open the dialog box that lets you personalize fax settings.

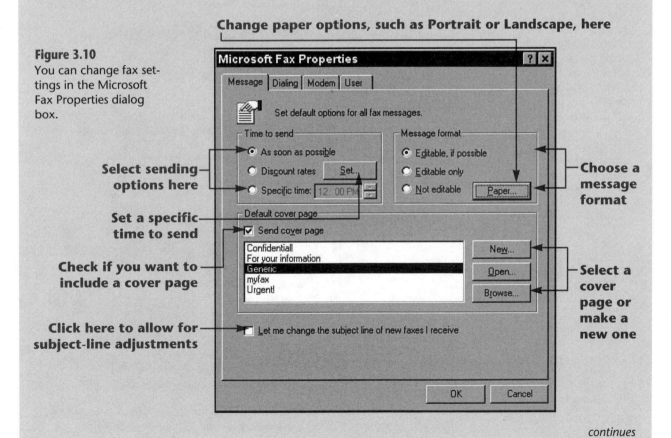

Figure 3.10
You can change fax settings in the Microsoft Fax Properties dialog box.

continues

To Set Up Your Fax   (continued)

③ Verify that the time to send is set to As Soon as Possible.

You can also set the fax to be delivered during discount rates or to be delivered at a specified time.

④ Verify that the message format is set to the Editable, if Possible option.

This feature allows a recipient with compatible equipment to edit the actual file, so they can work with the file directly on the computer. You can set other options in this area, such as paper orientation.

⑤ Select the Send Cover Page check box and verify that the default cover page is set to Generic.

In this example, choose the Generic fax cover page. You can choose the cover page you want by clicking to select it. Click New if you want to create a new cover sheet.

⑥ Choose the Dialog tab of the Microsoft Fax Properties dialog box (see Figure 3.11).

This page holds options for dialing properties, so that you can set the phone properties in the way you need.

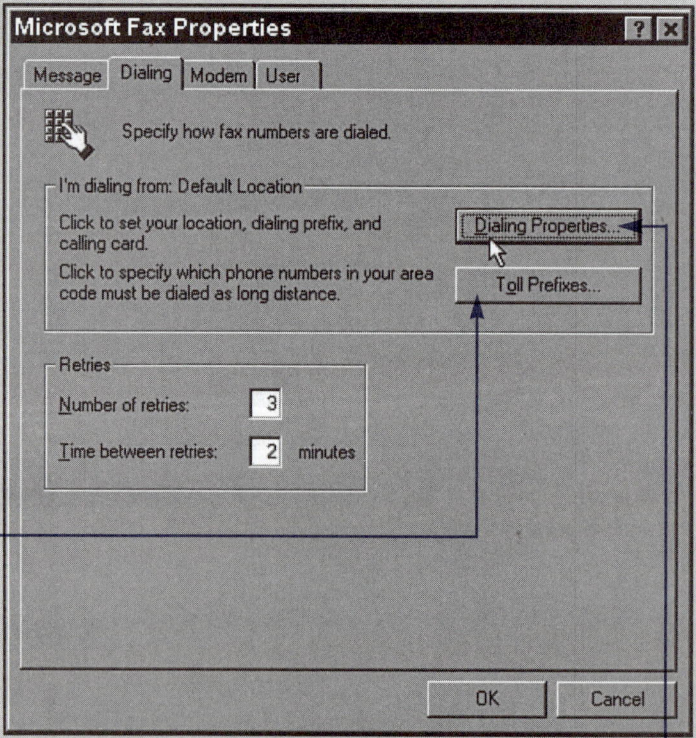

Figure 3.11
Change information about where you are calling from, phone-service features you want to use, specify which phone numbers in your area code must be dialed as long distance, and set how many times the fax will try to connect.

Click here to control local dialing parameters

Click here to change dialing properties, such as your dialing prefix or calling card information

Lesson 5: Sending a Fax   65

7 **Click the Dialing Properties button.**

The Dialing Properties dialog box appears and opens to the My Location tab. The information you fill in here automatically appears in the faxes you create. The My Location tab holds specific dialing information. Fill in your dialing properties. Your instructor will advise you if you need to change any information in this dialog box.

8 **Click OK to close the Dialing Properties dialog box and return to the Microsoft Fax Properties dialog box.**

9 **Click the Modem tab of the Microsoft Fax Properties dialog box.**

Your modem should be configured correctly, as in the earlier lesson.

10 **Click the User tab of the Microsoft Fax Properties dialog box.**

This information serves as default information for fax cover pages. Verify its accuracy before you proceed to the next lesson. Click OK to close the dialog box and accept any changes you have made.

You can also open Microsoft Exchange through the Start menu by selecting Programs, then choosing Microsoft Exchange.

It is more economical to create faxes and e-mail while offline because most online services charge incrementally for time spent accessing the service. Create and send all correspondence offline. Then log on to Microsoft Network and your messages will be automatically forwarded without your intervention. You can simultaneously send a fax to recipients using different services. For example, you can simultaneously send a fax to an individual using Microsoft Network and also copy to an individual who is using a stand-alone fax.

Lesson 5: Sending a Fax

Now that your fax settings are correct, you can send a fax directly from your computer. Follow the steps below to send a fax now.

To Send a Fax

1 **Double-click the Inbox icon on your desktop.**

You send faxes as well as e-mail in Microsoft Exchange because Microsoft Exchange is the central processing location for all incoming communications.

continues

Project 3 Printing, Modems, and Faxing

To Send a Fax (continued)

2 Choose Compose, New Fax.

This opens the Compose New Fax Wizard, as shown in Figure 3.12. There are two ways to address your outgoing fax: you can choose to type the name in the To text box or click Address Book to select the recipient's name from your Address Book.

3 Type the name of the person you are sending the fax to in the To text box (this is the recipient) for this lesson.

Ask your instructor for the correct fax recipient information. If you have multiple recipients, click Add to List to continue adding names to the Recipient List.

4 Enter the rest of the information, such as Country and Fax #.

Ask your instructor what fax number to use for this exercise.

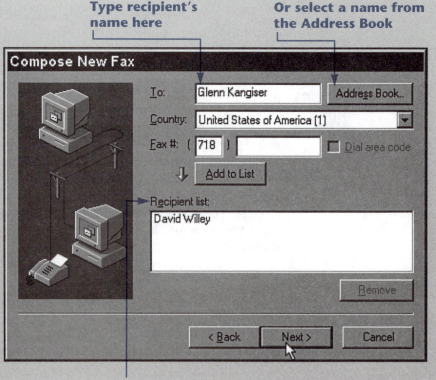

Figure 3.12
The Compose New Fax Wizard prompts you for the information it needs to compose new faxes.

5 Click Next.

The next screen of the Compose New Fax Wizard allows you to choose a cover page. You can also change your options if you need to through this box.

6 Click Next.

Type the Subject and any note you want to add on the cover sheet in this box. Select whether you want to include a note directly on the cover page.

7 Click Next to reach the next screen that deals with inserting files into the actual fax.

Use this screen if you want to include a file in the fax. You can only do this if the type of fax machine you are delivering to is compatible. To add a file, click Add File and continue.

8 Click Next.

This is the final screen of the Compose New Fax Wizard before sending the fax. Click the Back key to make any necessary changes before transmitting the fax.

9 Click Finish.

Microsoft Exchange sends the fax.

If you have problems...

If you are using an external modem, verify that the modem is connected to the phone jack and that any external cables are fully connected.

Check fax settings, as described in Lesson 4.

Lesson 6: Receiving Faxes

You can easily receive faxes from fax machines, fax-on-demand systems, and other fax-information services while working on your computer. You can retrieve faxes by using the Request a Fax Wizard from either the Fax Tools options on the Accessories menu or in Microsoft Exchange in a variety of ways.

If you are receiving a fax from a **Group 3** fax machine, you can retrieve editable files, or files you can edit, software updates, and fax images via fax. You will also need to have a Group 3-compatible modem. In this lesson, you use each method of retrieving a fax to become familiar with the available options.

68   Project 3   Printing, Modems, and Faxing

Jargon Watch

There are several different groups of fax modems and fax machines available to end users. Newer models have more capabilities than older machines, and they transfer data at a quicker rate than older models.

A **Group 3** fax machine can send and receive editable files (you or the recipient can open the fax and make changes, if necessary).

To Receive Faxes

1 In Microsoft Exchange, choose Tools, Microsoft Fax Tools, Request a Fax.

This is the same method you used in the first lesson to select Microsoft Fax Tools.

The Request a Fax Wizard appears to help you through the steps to download faxes, as shown in Figure 3.13.

Figure 3.13
Use the Request a Fax Wizard to quickly receive all faxes sent to you.

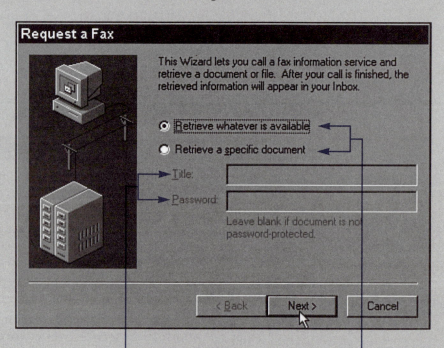

Tell the Wizard if you want all faxes or just a certain fax retrieved

If you want a file retrieved that is password-protected, type the title and password

Lesson 6:   Receiving Faxes   69

② Accept the default option, Retrieve Whatever is Available.

If you want to retrieve only one document, select Retrieve a Specific Document. When you use this option, you need to know the title of the document (and type it in the Title text box). If the document is password-protected, you need to type the password in the Password text box. Ignore this text box if you are retrieving a document that is not password-protected.

③ Click Next.

The next screen in the Request a Fax Wizard prompts you for the phone number and country you want to retrieve the fax from. It does this because you are requesting a fax from a particular location, not just picking up incoming faxes from your Inbox.

④ Type the name of the sender in the To box, or select a name by clicking the Address Book button.

⑤ Select the calling preference As Soon As Possible.

You can retrieve your fax immediately, when phone rates are discounted, or at a specific time.

⑥ Click Next.

Your faxes are ready to retrieve.

⑦ Click Finish to receive your fax now.

The faxes are downloaded.

If you don't ask to receive a fax, any faxes that have been sent to you since the last time you logged on to Microsoft Network will appear in your Inbox. You can easily retrieve and edit these faxes.

⑧ Double-click the fax message your instructor asks you to retrieve from your Microsoft Exchange Inbox.

There should be a fax in your Inbox. If you don't see an incoming fax, ask you instructor where you should look for the incoming fax. When you retrieve and view faxes, you might see an icon next to the fax (or e-mail) message. This icon indicates that a document is attached to the incoming fax. You can open the document by double-clicking the icon. This opens the Fax Viewer screen, as shown in Figure 3.14.

continues

Project 3 Printing, Modems, and Faxing

To Receive Faxes (continued)

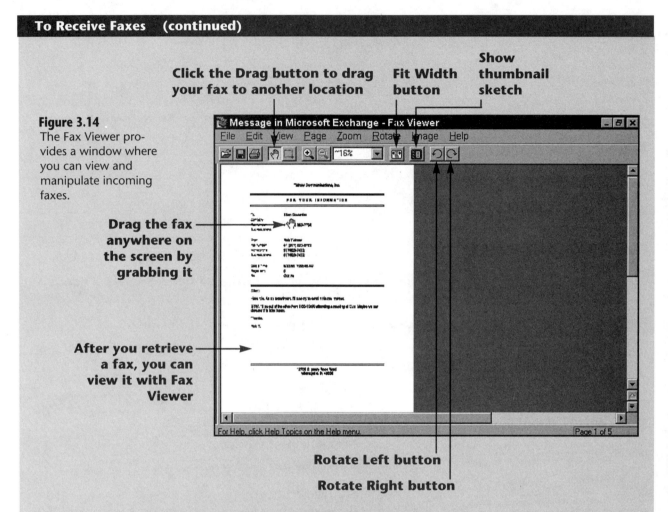

Figure 3.14
The Fax Viewer provides a window where you can view and manipulate incoming faxes.

9 Choose Edit, Drag.

You also can choose the Drag button on the toolbar, if you prefer.

10 Drag the fax document to any location on the screen.

You also can use the vertical and horizontal scroll bars to navigate around the screen. Follow the rest of these instructions to open another fax in Fax Viewer.

11 Choose File, Open.

Fax Viewer also shows outgoing fax messages that have been queued to send.

12 Select the fax you need to open, and click Open.

Fax Viewer allows you to manipulate your fax. Table 3.2 lists some unfamiliar button features of the Fax Viewer toolbar. Familiar buttons, such as Print, are skipped in this lesson.

If you prefer to open your faxes in Microsoft Exchange, you can double-click to open the fax you choose, as you did earlier in this project.

Lesson 6: Receiving Faxes

Table 3.2	Fax Viewer Features
Button	Description
Drag	Drags a fax anywhere on the current screen.
Select	Toggles the Selection tool on and off.
Fit Width	Fills the width of the screen.
Show Thumbnails	Toggles thumbnails of the fax on and off.
Rotate Left	Rotates the fax 90 degrees to the left.
Rotate Right	Rotates the fax 90 degrees to the right.

When you create a new message in Microsoft Exchange, you can add a name to your Address Book and make it available whenever you send a fax.

In this example, select yourself. Use your fax number and take this opportunity to add your name to the Address Book if you haven't already done so. Your name will then be available for a **blind cc** (a blind copy that is not noted for the original recipient of the document) if you want.

If Microsoft Exchange is open and your Fax button is available on the right corner of your Taskbar, click the Fax button to receive a fax. Just click the **A**nswer Now button.

You can also click the Start menu, select **P**rograms, Accessories, then choose Fax and Request a Fax.

You can also open a file in most Microsoft applications by pressing and holding down Ctrl, then pressing O.

If you have problems...

If you have a problem faxing, you might need to adjust a modem or property setting. Use the Sending and Receiving Faxes Troubleshooter to work through the possible causes. The Sending and Receiving Faxes Troubleshooter covers the most likely issues that might occur while sending and receiving faxes.

You access the Troubleshooter in Microsoft Exchange. Choose Help, Microsoft Fax Help Topics. Open the Index page by clicking the Index tab. Type **trouble** in the #1 box. The word Troubleshooting becomes selected in box #2. Click the Display button to open the Troubleshooter.

The Troubleshooter is an excellent source to use for assistance when faxing. However, if you have an external modem, you should first make sure that the cable that connects the modem to the communications port is connected. You can also turn your modem off, then turn it back on. This clears the modem and returns its settings to the defaults.

Project 3 Printing, Modems, and Faxing

To Print A Fax

❶ Choose File, Print.

Use this procedure if you have the fax open in Microsoft Exchange. You can also click the Printer button on the toolbar.

Lesson 7: Working with Dial-Up Networking

Network server is a computer configured to serve multiple users, computers, and requests.

If you do not have a portable computer available, but do have a home computer, Windows 95 offers another tool, Dial-Up Networking. Dial-Up Networking allows you to access your company's **network server**, even if your home computer is not on a network. Both computers must, however, have modems.

The first thing you need to know is how to set up a connection from your computer to the network computer. Follow these steps to bring up the Dial-Up Networking Wizard to guide you through the connection process.

Connecting to a Remote Network

❶ Double-click My Computer on your desktop.

If you do not have a Dial-Up Networking icon in My Computer, it is not installed. Ask your Administrator to install it so you can proceed.

❷ Double-click Dial-Up Networking.

The Dial-Up Networking window opens.

❸ Double-click Make New Connection to start the Dial-Up Networking Wizard.

The Wizard appears and prompts you to answer questions that allow the computers to connect (see Figure 3.15).

To dial a connection that you have already set up, double-click its icon in the Dial-Up Networking window instead of the Make New Connection icon.

Lesson 7: Working with Dial-Up Networking   73

Figure 3.15
Connect to a Remote Network with Dial-Up Networking.

Type the computer name you are dialing

Verify the modem or select another

Fine-tune modem properties

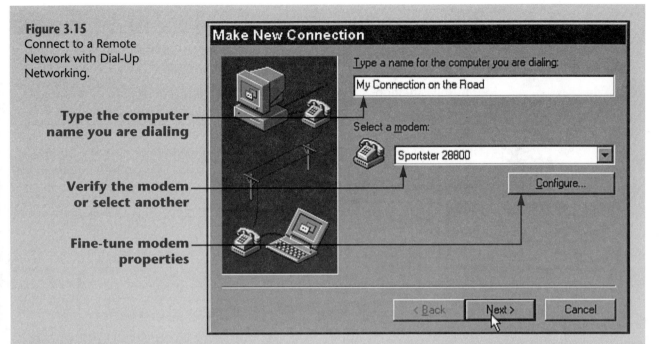

④ Type a name for the computer you are dialing.

Your instructor will tell you what number will be used for this exercise. This screen will also show the attached modem type. You only need to configure this if you recently installed a new modem.

⑤ Click Next if you do not need to configure the modem type.

You move to the next Wizard screen.

⑥ Verify that you are working in the correct connection.

Verify the phone number and country code for the location you are dialing. You can click Back at any time to change a setting.

⑦ Fill in any options that are not filled in.

All settings should be filled in before continuing your Dial-up Connection. Portions might already be pre-configured by your Systems Administrator.

⑧ Click Next.

The final screen tells you the name of the successful connection you have created and provides you with options, depending on what you want to do next. Double-click Finish if you want to connect to the computer at this time. Single-click Finish to simply save the connection for future use.

This information tells the computer certain criteria so that it can recognize when it locates the correct computer.

⑨ Notice the new icon in your Dial-Up Networking window with the connection name you applied.

This connection will remain available for future use.

74 Project 3 Printing, Modems, and Faxing

> **If You Have Problems...**
>
> Occasionally, the international business traveler might have difficulty connecting. This is caused by different country codes and system differences.
>
> In this situation, you can manually dial up your connection. Use the following steps when you need to connect to another network manually.

There are several ways to access Dial-Up Networking. Right-click My Computer, and choose Open. This opens My Computer. Locate Dial-Up Networking in the folder listings, and double-click to open.

Right-click the Start menu and select Explore. Double-click Dial-up Network in the left panel of Windows Explorer.

To Manually Dial a Dial-Up Connection

1 **Right-click the Start button and choose Explore.**

This opens Windows Explorer. In the left panel, scroll until you see Dial-Up Networking.

2 **Double-click Dial-Up Networking.**

The Dial-Up Networking folder appears.

3 **In the Dial-Up Networking folder, select the connection you want to change, then choose File, Properties. Your instructor will provide the connection name you will use for these steps.**

The General tab of the My Connection Properties dialog box appears (see Figure 3.16).

4 **Click the Configure button and select the Options tab from the Properties dialog box that appears. You only change one option on this page.**

Lesson 7: Working with Dial-Up Networking

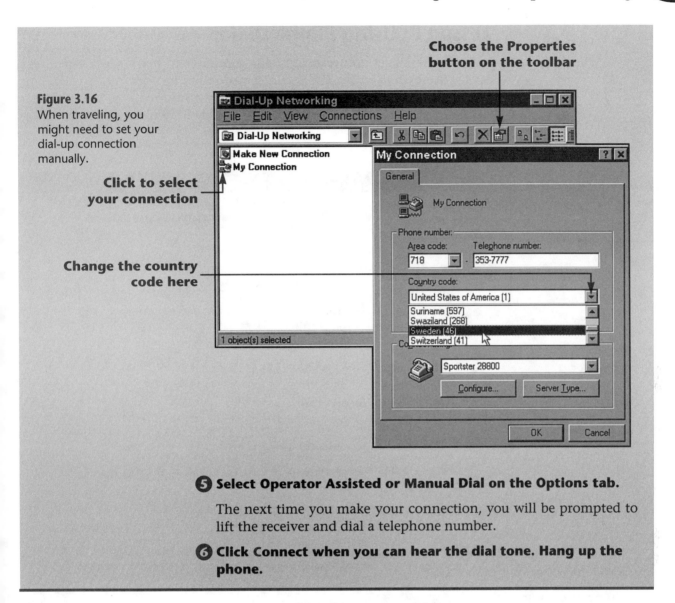

Figure 3.16
When traveling, you might need to set your dial-up connection manually.

⑤ Select Operator Assisted or Manual Dial on the Options tab.

The next time you make your connection, you will be prompted to lift the receiver and dial a telephone number.

⑥ Click Connect when you can hear the dial tone. Hang up the phone.

Project 3 Printing, Modems, and Faxing

Lesson 8: Using Phone Dialer

With Phone Dialer, you can use your computer to make voice telephone calls. Phone Dialer uses the settings you made in your modem Dialing Properties for calling card and dialing location information. You can also use Phone Dialer in conjunction with your dedicated fax machine to log faxes.

To Use Phone Dialer

1 Click Start, choose Programs, Accessories, Phone Dialer.

The phone dialer appears.

2 Type the phone number in the Number To Dial list box.

This number will be given to you by your instructor and needs to be entered in dialable format (use the dashes). You can also use a number you have previously dialed.

3 Click Dial.

The call is initiated.

4 Choose Tools, Show Log.

You can log telephone calls with Phone Dialer from the Tools menu. The Call Log dialog box appears.

5 Choose Edit, Speed Dial in the Phone Dialer dialog box (see Fig. 3.17).

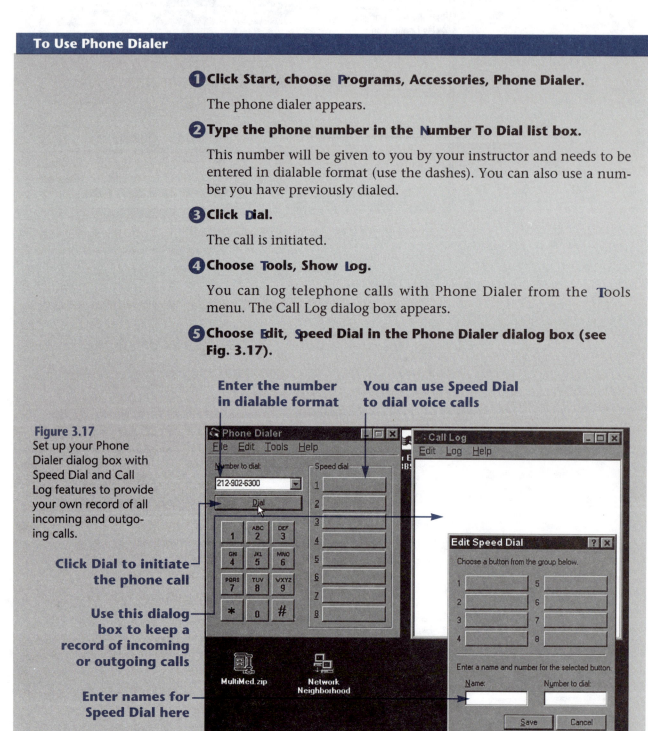

Figure 3.17
Set up your Phone Dialer dialog box with Speed Dial and Call Log features to provide your own record of all incoming and outgoing calls.

Store phone numbers that you dial frequently on a speed dial button.

You can dial a number in your call log. To see your call log, click Tools and choose Show Log. If you want to use that number to dial, double-click the phone number.

To edit all of your speed-dial buttons at once, such as purging numbers, choose **E**dit, **S**peed Dial.

You can select whether you want to log incoming or outgoing calls by choosing Log, Options.

Project Summary

To	Do This
Set up a printer	Click **S**tart, and choose **S**ettings, **P**rinters; double-click the Add Printer button to start the wizard.
Set up a modem	Click **S**tart, and choose **S**ettings, **C**ontrol Panel; double-click Modems; click Add and follow the wizard instructions.
Connect to another computer with HyperTerminal	Click Start, and choose **P**rograms, Accessories, HyperTerminal, double-click the server icon; click OK, OK, Dial.
Set up a new connection with HyperTerminal	Choose **F**ile, **N**ew Connection; type the service name; click OK.
Set fax options	Double-click the Inbox, choose **T**ools, Microsoft Fa**x** Tools, **O**ptions, adjust tabs as needed.
Send a fax	Double-click Inbox, click Co**m**pose, New Fa**x**, follow the Wizard's instructions.
Retrieve a Fax	Double-click Inbox, click **T**ools, Microsoft Fa**x** Tools, **R**equest a Fax, select what you want to retrieve, and follow the Wizard's instructions.
View a fax	Double-click the fax in Inbox.
Print a fax	Choose **F**ile, **P**rint, or select the Printer icon from the toolbar.
Connecting to a remote network	Double-click My Computer, Dial-Up Networking, select Make New Connection, and follow the Wizard's instructions.
Use Phone Dialer	Click Start, **P**rograms, Accessories, Phone Dialer type the phone number, click **D**ial.

Applying Your Skills

1. Change from your current default printer to another printer in your department. Make sure you set the printer as a default. Print a test page.

2. Set up a modem for another user in the class. If you can reset your modem to another modem, do so in this exercise, in addition to setting another user's modem.

3. Set up to connect to a remote computer in your department that does not use Windows 95. Ask your Administrator or instructor what computer to use. The method you should use for this exercise is HyperTerminal. Transfer a file to verify the successful connection.

4. Set your fax settings, then send a test fax to a co-worker in class. Troubleshoot any problems through the Troubleshooter in Help. Use a fellow student and have them return the fax to you with a response.

5. Repeat step 3 of Applying your Skills, but this time use Dial-Up Networking to connect to a computer that uses Windows 95. Your instructor may provide you with information so you can transfer a file to verify the successful connection.

6. Set up your most-used phone numbers in Speed Dial.

Project

4

Getting the Most from Windows 95 Help

Objectives

In this project, you learn how to

➤ Find a Topic in Help

➤ Copy Information from a Help Topic

➤ Print a Help Topic

➤ Add Comments to Help Topics

➤ Get Help in a Dialog Box

➤ Change the Font Size of a Help Topic

➤ Change System Colors in a Help Topic

➤ Browse Help for Similar Topics

Project 4 Getting the Most from Windows 95 Help

Why Would I Do This?

Often when people begin working in a new operating system, they enjoy the features, but eventually delve into a feature a little more deeply and become confused. That can be frustrating if you don't have the appropriate help available. But that's not a problem in Windows 95; Windows 95 empowers you to help yourself and troubleshoot your own questions.

In this project, you find solutions to questions, and you find out where to get tips. You learn how to copy, print, and annotate in Help, change the way Help looks, search for similar topics, and get help on the fly. This project takes you through the full range of features in Windows Help.

Lesson 1: Finding a Topic in Help

Windows 95 makes help available to you from any screen you work in. You can access help from the Start menu as soon as you begin working in Windows 95. There are several ways to approach Help. You might prefer to look just for the topic that comes to mind. You might have an hour to follow step-by-step procedures on topics that interest you. You set the pace. Take the following steps to view the Help options available to you.

To Find a Topic in Help

1 Click Start.

When you were first introduced to Help, you accessed it through My Computer because you were becoming familiar with My Computer. But you can also get Help directly from the Start button.

2 Click Help.

You used the Settings menu in past projects. Now, use the Help menu to familiarize yourself with how Microsoft Help is set up, and to see what interface you prefer. The Help Topics dialog box opens to the Contents tab by default (see Fig. 4.1).

Lesson 1: Finding a Topic in Help   81

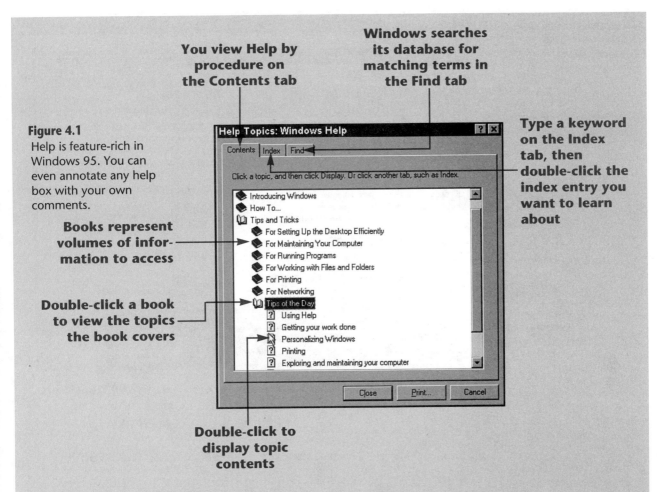

Figure 4.1
Help is feature-rich in Windows 95. You can even annotate any help box with your own comments.

You view Help by procedure on the Contents tab

Windows searches its database for matching terms in the Find tab

Type a keyword on the Index tab, then double-click the index entry you want to learn about

Books represent volumes of information to access

Double-click a book to view the topics the book covers

Double-click to display topic contents

❸ Double-click Troubleshooting.

Troubleshooting is listed alphabetically after Tips and Tricks. You might have to scroll to see it. You can also single-click Troubleshooting and choose **O**pen (the Close button changes to Open—if you have an item open, the button provides the option to Close). The menu expands to list the troubleshooters that are available.

❹ Double-click `If you have trouble using your modem.`

The Modem Troubleshooter appears with a brief explanation about what to expect, as shown in Figure 4.2. The Troubleshooter then provides a list of questions to interactively walk you through to find the solution to your problem.

continues

To Find a Topic in Help   (continued)

Figure 4.2
Troubleshooters anticipate problems that might occur and help you to solve them by yourself.

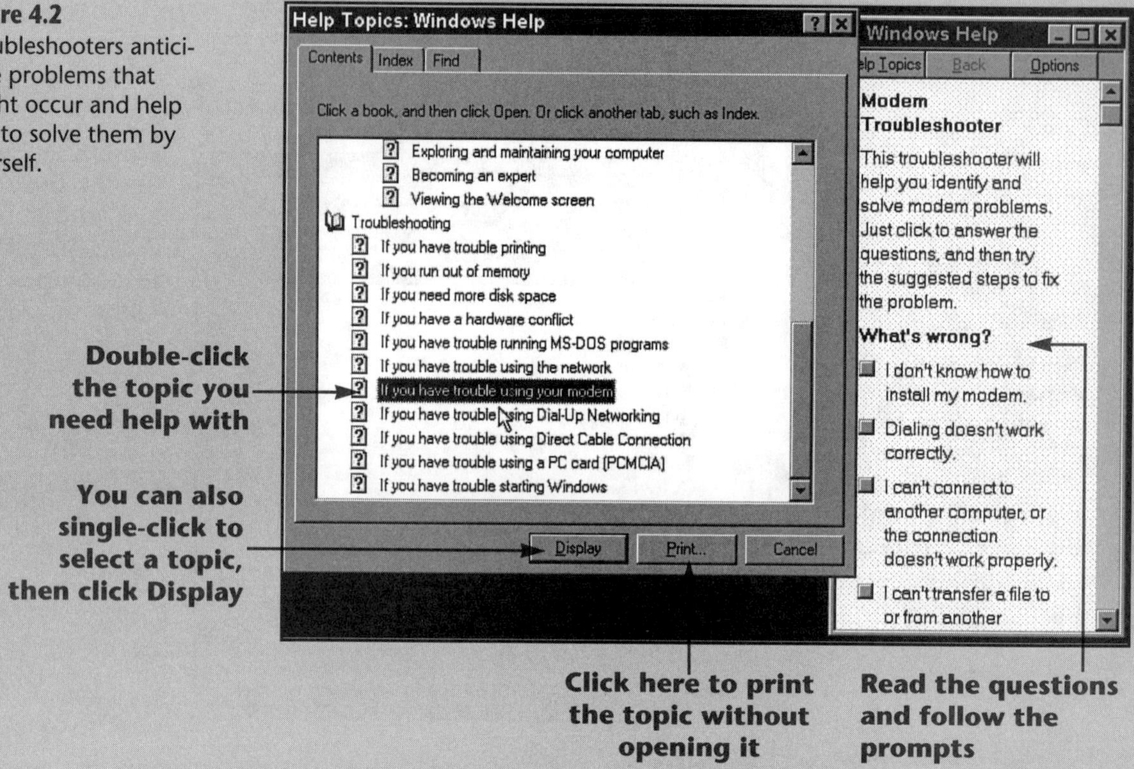

Double-click the topic you need help with

You can also single-click to select a topic, then click Display

Help Topics: Windows Help

Contents | Index | Find

Click a book, and then click Open. Or click another tab, such as Index.

- [?] Exploring and maintaining your computer
- [?] Becoming an expert
- [?] Viewing the Welcome screen
- Troubleshooting
  - [?] If you have trouble printing
  - [?] If you run out of memory
  - [?] If you need more disk space
  - [?] If you have a hardware conflict
  - [?] If you have trouble running MS-DOS programs
  - [?] If you have trouble using the network
  - [?] If you have trouble using your modem
  - [?] If you have trouble using Dial-Up Networking
  - [?] If you have trouble using Direct Cable Connection
  - [?] If you have trouble using a PC card (PCMCIA)
  - [?] If you have trouble starting Windows

Display | Print... | Cancel

Windows Help

Help Topics | Back | Options

Modem Troubleshooter

This troubleshooter will help you identify and solve modem problems. Just click to answer the questions, and then try the suggested steps to fix the problem.

What's wrong?

- I don't know how to install my modem.
- Dialing doesn't work correctly.
- I can't connect to another computer, or the connection doesn't work properly.
- I can't transfer a file to or from another

Click here to print the topic without opening it

Read the questions and follow the prompts

⑤ In the Modem Troubleshooter dialog box, click Help Topics.

This returns you to the main menu containing the three access tabs for referral. There are other ways to find help with any question you have about Windows 95. Now use the Index tab to find help with your modem.

⑥ Click the Index tab.

The Index tab is set up by items listed in the Index of Windows 95 instructions.

⑦ Type modem in the Type the First Few Letters of the Word You're Looking For text box.

This tab is a different view of **H**elp (see Fig. 4.3). There are two areas: type the topic in step one and notice step two searches for all items that pertain to the item you typed in step 1. If you are interested only in using a modem with your fax, you can click that topic and get help.

Lesson 1: Finding a Topic in Help

Figure 4.3
The Index tab looks at all Index entries and displays a list that matches your search word.

As you type, any index entries matching the word(s) you type are displayed

Type the index entry you want to see in this box

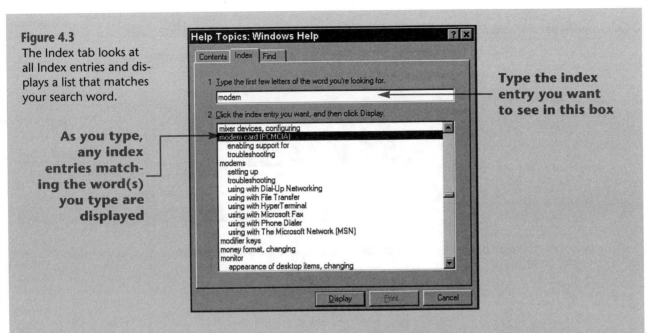

8. **Double-click Using with Microsoft Fax in the Click the Index Entry You Want, and then Click Display list box (step 2).**

   Help about using Microsoft Fax appears. You can find help on any topic using the same method. Click the Help Topics button to return to the Index tab.

   You might want to search for any information about a topic, not just Index entries. You can find all instances of a certain word or phrase in Windows 95 Help by using the Find tab.

9. **Click the Find tab.**

10. **Enter the text fax modem in the Type the Word(s) You Want to Find text box.**

    The results will look similar to Figure 4.4. You can personalize Find tab options. If, for example, your screen does not look like Figure 4.4, you can change the way Find searches.

    continues

To Find a Topic in Help (continued)

Figure 4.4
If you use the Find tab, you can just type in the word you want to see references about, and Help will display titles of all matching Help windows.

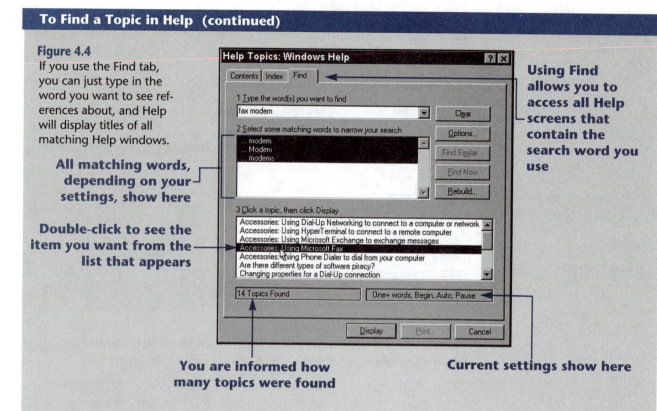

Using Find allows you to access all Help screens that contain the search word you use

All matching words, depending on your settings, show here

Double-click to see the item you want from the list that appears

You are informed how many topics were found

Current settings show here

⓫ Click the Options button.

The Find Options dialog box appears. Make sure that At Least One of The Words You Typed button is selected (see Fig. 4.5). Click OK to return to the Find tab of the Help Topics dialog box.

Figure 4.5
You can change the way Windows searches for words when using the Find tab in Help through options available in the Find Options dialog box.

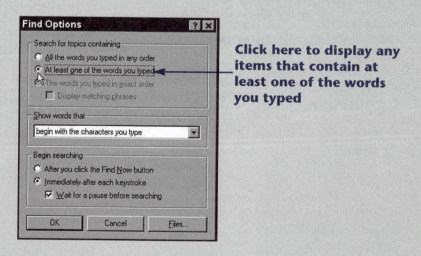

Click here to display any items that contain at least one of the words you typed

⓬ Select Accessories: Using Microsoft Fax, then click the Display button to view the contents.

Close all Help boxes when you finish with this lesson before proceeding to the next lesson.

Lesson 1: Finding a Topic in Help 85

Table 4.1 describes the Contents tab of the Help Topics dialog box. You can brief yourself about changes in Windows 95, use How To, check out the Tips and Tricks, or solve a current problem with the Troubleshooter.

Table 4.1	The Contents Tab
Element	Function
If You've Used Windows Before	Click to select, click Display to open a tour of the changes in Windows 95 and to find out where to find items that are familiar to you (see Fig. 4.6).
Introducing Windows	Gives an introduction to Windows, providing information by general category, such as Using Windows Accessories "For Writing and Drawing" or "For Sound and Video."
How To	How do I do this? Here's where you find the answer to that question. Topics include Work with Files and Folders, and Use a Network.
Tips and Tricks	You find shortcuts and time savers in this section.
Troubleshooting	If you are running into a problem with a procedure or hardware, check here for interactive troubleshooters.

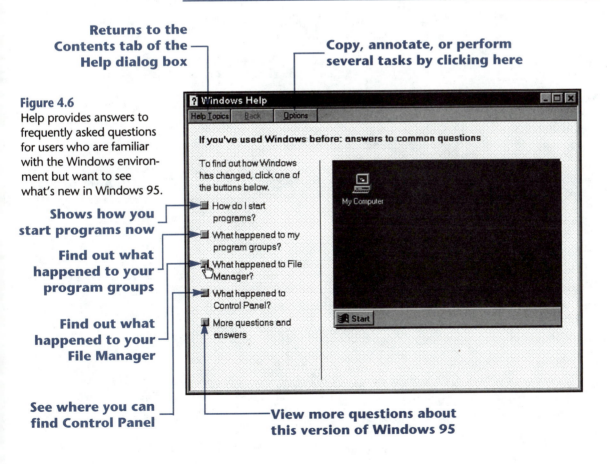

Figure 4.6
Help provides answers to frequently asked questions for users who are familiar with the Windows environment but want to see what's new in Windows 95.

86 Project 4 Getting the Most from Windows 95 Help

Lesson 2: Browsing Help for Similar Topics

You might not always know the exact word you are looking for. Without being prompted to search for "fax modem" in Lesson one, you might have decided to search using the word "modem." Depending on how your File Search feature has been configured, you might not be able to see the fax modem Help topic. In this lesson, you set up your Find tab to facilitate searching for similar topics.

To Browse Help for Similar Topics

❶ Click Start, and choose Help.

❷ Click the Find tab.

The Find tab contains a database of accessible information. You can personalize it, depending on your search needs.

❸ Type notes in the Type the Word(s) You Want to Find list box.

Look in the Click a Topic, Then Click Display list box. The sixth item down should be Adding Comments to a Help Topic.

❹ Select the Adding Comments to a Help Topic check box.

Notice the number of topics that are relevant to your search (see Fig. 4.7).

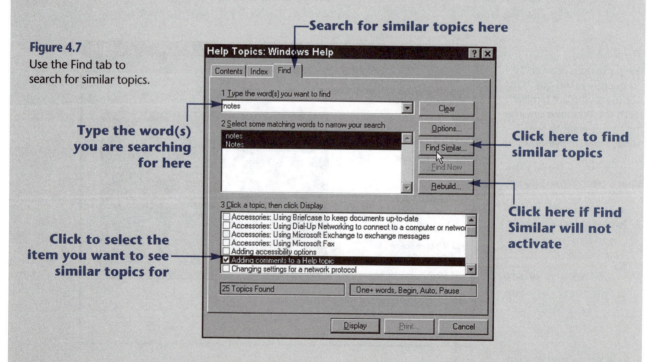

Figure 4.7
Use the Find tab to search for similar topics.

❺ Click Find Similar.

If the Find Similar button appears grayed out (or deselected), follow the steps in the following If You Have Problems section, then continue with these steps.

Lesson 3: Copying Information from a Help Topic 87

> **If you have problems...**
>
> The Find Similar button might not be available to you because of the way your Find database has been set up. Before setting up how Find uses your database, it is a good idea to decide how you will need to use Help. For the most success in finding what you are looking for, you will need to tell Windows 95 what you want your searches to look for. Click **R**ebuild to rebuild the search list and begin the wizard that assists you with setting your preferences. When the screen appears asking you to choose if you want to Customize Search Capabilities, select Support Similarity Searches, then finish the wizard prompts.

6 Repeat steps 3 through 5.

You only need to do this if you had to rebuild your search database. Otherwise, go to step 7.

7 Click to select the topic that interests you.

If many options appear, you can scroll to move around the box and read all topics available to you.

8 Click Display.

You can also double-click the topic to display it without having to click the Display button.

The searches you request when working in the Find tab are saved to provide you with a history of what you have looked up recently. This can save search time. Take a few minutes to type **modem**, select an item from the Click a Topic, Then Click Display, then click **D**isplay to display it. Now do the same with the word **printer**. After you finish these inquiries, click the arrow to the right of the Type the Word(s) You Want to Find list box. All topics you displayed are available to quickly use again if you want.

Lesson 3: Copying Information from a Help Topic

Have you ever had to toggle between a Help topic and your work window? By the time you get back to the window, you forget the next step you were supposed to take. In this lesson, you learn how you can actually put the instruction into your document, or make the Help dialog box stand on top of any open item so you can view the instructions as you follow the steps. You also learn the universal shortcut method for opening Help.

88 Project 4 Getting the Most from Windows 95 Help

To Copy Information from a Help Topic

❶ Press F1 from your desktop.

This is another way to access Help. You don't need to have anything open on your desktop to initiate Help, not even the Start button. The Help dialog box appears and displays the last tab you were using.

If you have problems...

If the Taskbar is currently activated, you will not be able to initiate Help from the desktop by pressing F1. If this happens, click anywhere on the desktop once to deactivate the taskbar. Try again.

❷ Double-click the Tips and Tricks book.

Files that contain tips and tricks expand from the book.

❸ Double-click For Printing.

You can put a shortcut to your printer on your desktop to speed up your printing time. Who doesn't want to make printing go faster?

❹ Double-click Putting a Shortcut To a Printer on the Desktop.

This opens a new panel that shows you how to put a printer icon on your desktop.

❺ Click Options to open the menu shown in Figure 4.8.

By default, Help dialog boxes are kept on top of the active window, but you might not want it to be on top.

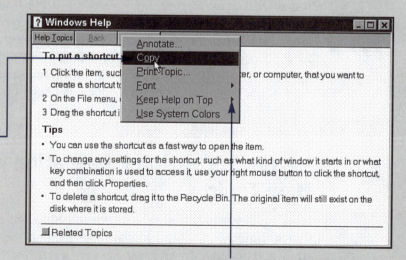

Figure 4.8
Through Options, you copy Help text and control how Help appears on your screen.

Click Copy to copy the contents of a Help dialog box

Click Keep Help on Top to force the Help dialog box to remain on top of all open applications

Lesson 4: Printing a Help Topic **89**

6 Choose Keep Help on Top.

You can choose Not on Top to allow you to see other applications, such as your word processor, without having Help in the way while you work.

7 Choose Not on Top.

8 Open Wordpad now and maximize it. You should not see the Help window (even though it is currently open) because you have set the options so that Help is not always on top.

9 Click the Windows Help button on the Taskbar.

This activates the current Help window and displays it on top of Wordpad. Do not click in Wordpad, or the Help window will disappear again.

10 In the Help window, choose Options.

You are going to copy the entire Help topic.

11 Choose Copy.

The text of the current Help window is copied. Now paste it into Wordpad.

12 Select Paste in your word processor.

You can also press Ctrl+V to paste the text where you want it. The directions from the Help dialog box are pasted directly into your document, so that you can follow them as you proceed.

13 Close Help.

You can close Help by clicking the Close button on the title bar.

Sometimes, you'll get into a Help dialog box that doesn't have the Options button, so you can't choose the Copy command. You can still copy the information contained in the dialog box. Right-click inside the dialog box. Choose Copy from the submenu that appears.

If you only want to copy a portion of the topic, click and drag to select what you want to copy, then click Copy.

Lesson 4: Printing a Help Topic

There are times when it is easier to print a Help topic. Perhaps a coworker needs help. You can print out any Help topic to use a hard copy of the information. In this lesson, you practice printing Help topics.

90 Project 4 Getting the Most from Windows 95 Help

To Print a Help Topic

❶ Open Help by the method you prefer.

You've learned three ways to access help so far (two in this project).

❷ Double-click Introducing Windows.

The book opens and the tree expands, displaying a list of topics.

❸ Choose Using Windows Accessories.

The tree expands again.

❹ Double-click For Sound and Video.

This tree expands to show more options.

❺ Double-click CD Player for Playing Compact Discs.

The text for this procedure pops up.

❻ Click Options.

The Options drop-down menu opens, as you saw in the preceding lesson (see Fig. 4.9).

Figure 4.9
Print a hard copy of Help text using either the Options menu or by right-clicking in the Help screen.

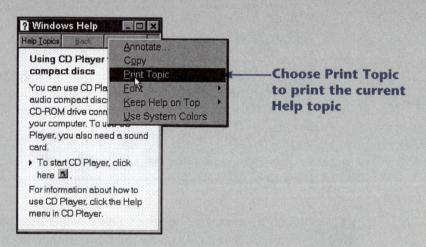

❼ Choose Print Topic.

The topic prints. You can print from Help without using the Options menu; try doing that in the following steps.

❽ Right-click in the text area of the Help dialog box.

A submenu appears with options you can select (see Fig. 4.10).

Lesson 5:   Adding Comments to Help Topics   91

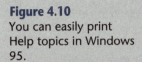

Figure 4.10
You can easily print Help topics in Windows 95.

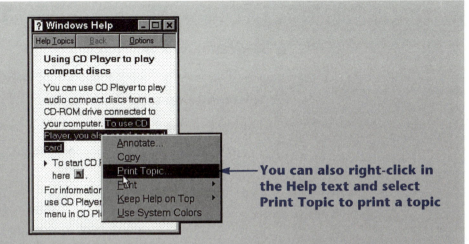

You can also right-click in the Help text and select Print Topic to print a topic

❾ Select Print Topic from the submenu.

The Help text for playing CD players prints. You see the topic print, but did you know you can print several topics from the Contents tab?

❿ Click Help Topics.

You return to the Contents tab.

⓫ Click Sound and Video.

⓬ Click the Close button.

This collapses the tree of topics. Remember, you can double-click if you want to.

⓭ Select Print from the Contents tab.

Windows prints the group of related topics stored in the Sound and Video tab. Close all Windows Help windows that are currently open in preparation for the next lesson.

Lesson 5: Adding Comments to Help Topics

You've looked up help topics in a variety of ways now. You can copy help text, print help text, and find help topics in the way most suited to you. But you can do even more with your Help feature. You can actually annotate your help text with your own comments for future reference. Perhaps a trainer has informed you of a shortcut that suits your company requirements, but which isn't described in Windows Help. You can add the tip to Help to make Help an even more robust aid. Practice personalizing Help now by adding annotations to it.

Project 4 Getting the Most from Windows 95 Help

To Add Comments to Help Topics

1 **Click Start, and choose Help.**

The Help feature opens; the Contents tab should be on top.

2 **Select the Find tab.**

The Find tab is where you will begin annotating a Help topic.

3 **Type annotate in the Type the Word(s) You Want to Find list box.**

Depending on your current Search option settings, you should see an Add Comments to a Help Topic option in the Click a Topic, Then Click Display list box. If you don't see the option, scroll through the list until it becomes visible.

4 **Select Add Comments to a Help topic.**

It might already be selected. Use this topic in this exercise to remind you of this feature.

5 **Choose Options, Annotate.**

If you prefer, you can right-click in the text to choose Annotate from the shortcut menu.

The Annotate dialog box appears, as shown in Figure 4.11. It is empty if you have not previously made notes on this topic. If you have made notes previously, they show in the Current Annotation list box.

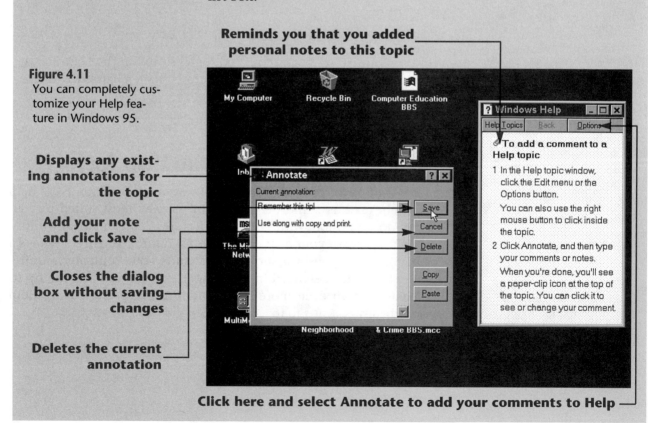

Figure 4.11
You can completely customize your Help feature in Windows 95.

Reminds you that you added personal notes to this topic

Displays any existing annotations for the topic

Add your note and click Save

Closes the dialog box without saving changes

Deletes the current annotation

Click here and select Annotate to add your comments to Help

Lesson 6: How to Get Help in a Dialog Box

6 **Type Pass this information to other Windows 95 users in the Current Annotation list box.**

Remember that you can also copy and paste. Or you can make any notation you choose.

7 **Look at the available buttons in the Annotate dialog box.**

You can cancel if you want to leave this box without saving any current changes. You can delete a current annotation. You can also copy and paste in this box.

8 **Click Save.**

The Annotate dialog box closes, and you now have a paper clip visible to the left of the Help topic. This is a reminder that you have added personal notes to this topic.

9 **Close Help.**

The next time you open Help, try one of the three methods you have learned so far: F1, Start, or My Computer. You can also open Help from the desktop by pressing Ctrl+Esc, then pressing H.

Lesson 6: How to Get Help in a Dialog Box

So far, you've learned a lot of ways to get the most out of the Help feature when you are using it from the Windows desktop. Sometimes, however, you might need help while working in a Windows dialog box. But a Help button is not always available in dialog boxes. This lesson teaches you how to get to Help, even in a dialog box.

To Get Help in a Dialog Box

1 **Click Start.**

Don't select Help. You will not be working in the Help dialog box for this exercise.

2 **Select Settings.**

You worked in the Control Panel for an earlier exercise on setting up your modem. Let's use Control Panel again for this exercise.

3 **Select Control Panel.**

The Control Panel opens up.

4 **Select the modem icon from Control Panel by double-clicking the icon.**

The Modems Properties dialog box appears, as shown in Figure 4.12. There is a question mark button on the title bar.

continues

To Get Help in a Dialog Box (continued)

Figure 4.12
Most dialog boxes feature a question mark on the Title bar; click it for help.

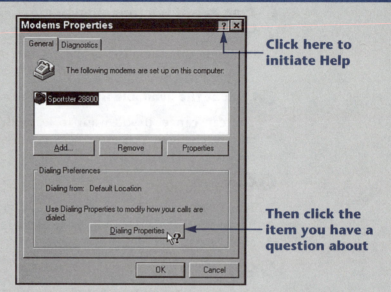

Click here to initiate Help

Then click the item you have a question about

5 **Click once on the Help button.**

The icon turns into a question mark. You can now get help on a topic by clicking the topic you are interested in.

6 **Click the Dialing Properties button.**

A brief description appears, describing the item you selected, as shown in Figure 4.13. When you finish reading the description, click anywhere on the screen to close the description box. Close all Help boxes now.

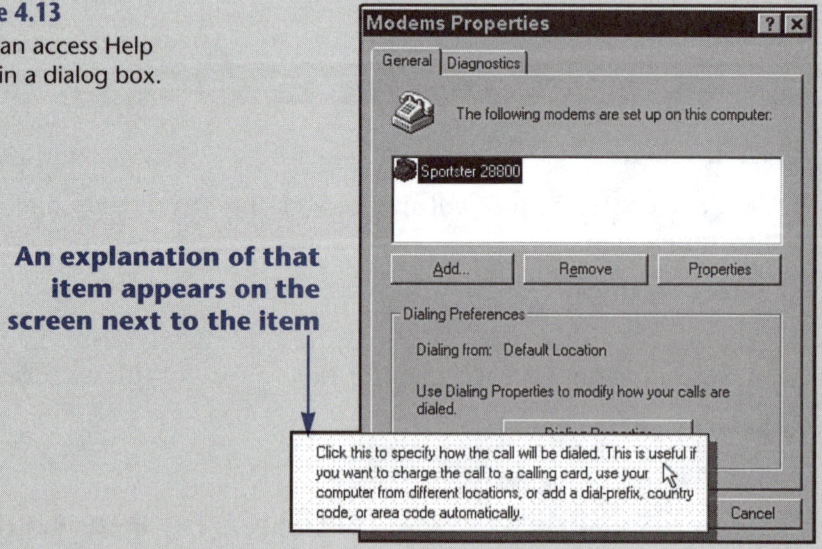

Figure 4.13
You can access Help even in a dialog box.

An explanation of that item appears on the screen next to the item

Lesson 7: Changing the Font Size of a Help Topic   95

 You can perform the same procedure with the F1 key. Tab through the dialog box until you select the area you have a question about. When that item is selected, press F1. The explanation pops up.

Click inside a pop-up box to close it.

Right-click an item in a dialog box. A What's This box appears. Click it, and the pop-up screen appears.

Lesson 7: Changing the Font Size of a Help Topic

If you want to see the text in the Help box in a different font size, you can adjust it while in Help. The change only lasts while that Help topic is open. It does not stay in effect once a Help topic changes.

To Change the Font Size of a Help Topic

❶ Press Ctrl+Esc, then press H.

This opens Help in Windows 95.

❷ Click the Contents tab.

❸ Double-click How To.

The tree expands with topics for help.

❹ Double-click Use a Network.

❺ Choose Browsing Your Workgroup from the options available.

❻ Select Options from the menu.

A drop-down menu appears, presenting more options to choose from (see Fig. 4.14).

❼ Select Font.

Another drop-down menu appears, presenting different font options.

Figure 4.14
The Options drop-down menu allows you to change the font size of your Help topic.

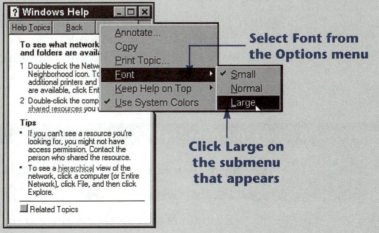

continues

Project 4 Getting the Most from Windows 95 Help

To Change the Font Size of a Help Topic (continued)

8 **Choose Large from the choices available.**

You can choose between Small, Normal, and Large. The font size changes; in this case, the Help dialog box enlarges to accommodate the larger font, as shown in Figure 4.15.

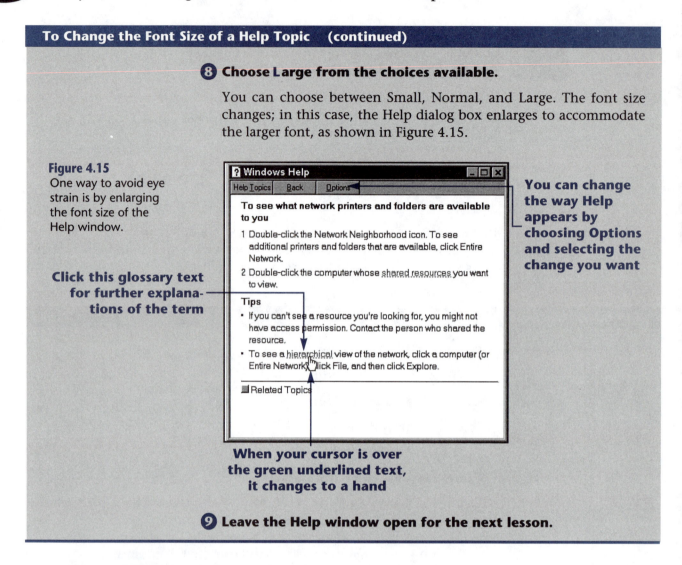

Figure 4.15
One way to avoid eye strain is by enlarging the font size of the Help window.

Click this glossary text for further explanations of the term

You can change the way Help appears by choosing Options and selecting the change you want

When your cursor is over the green underlined text, it changes to a hand

9 **Leave the Help window open for the next lesson.**

Remember that you can also right-click anywhere in the Help text to open the Options drop-down menu.

Lesson 8: Changing System Colors in a Help Topic

When you initiate Help, the dialog box that appears does not have the same system colors that you work in. You can change these colors to match your work screen. The following exercise shows you how easy it is to change system colors. You should still be in the Browsing Your Workgroup dialog box for this exercise.

To Change System Colors in a Help Topic

1 **Right-click in the text area of the Help dialog box.**

2 **Click Use System Colors.**

A dialog box appears to inform you that you can change system colors only if you close Help and restart it (see Fig. 4.16).

Lesson 8: Changing System Colors in a Help Topic

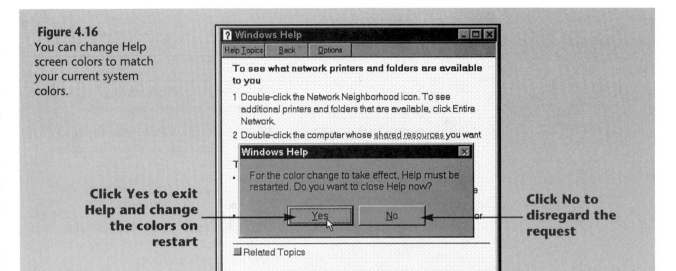

Figure 4.16
You can change Help screen colors to match your current system colors.

Click Yes to exit Help and change the colors on restart

Click No to disregard the request

❸ Click Yes.

Help closes. You must now restart Help for the new color scheme to take effect.

❹ Click Start, and choose Help.

When Help starts again, the background color and the text will be the same as the color choices you have set for your computer.

❺ Click the Contents tab.

❻ Double-click How To.

The tree expands with topics for help.

❼ Double-click Use a Network, and choose Browsing Your Workgroup.

Your screens should now be in the correct system colors.

❽ Close Help.

You can close help by clicking the Close button on the title bar.

If you have problems...

You might be working in Help after you change your system colors, then click a different Help topic, and your screen returns to the old setting. You have done nothing incorrectly. When you change the system color in Windows 95 Help, it affects only the current Help topic, the same way changing the font to another size only affects the current Help topic.

Project Summary

To	Do This
Find a topic in Help	Click Start, **H**elp, choose the tab you want, double-click to select a topic.
Copy information from a Help topic	In the Help topic you want to copy, select **O**ptions, **C**opy; click **P**aste in the application.
Print a Help topic	In the Help topic you want to print, select **O**ptions, **P**rint or **P**rint Topic.
Annotate a Help topic	In the Help topic you want to add a note to, select **O**ptions, **A**nnotate. Type in the Annotate box, click **S**ave.
Get Help in a Dialog box	Click the question mark button on the Title bar and select the item you want information about.
Change Help font size	In the Help topic you want to change the font size on, select **O**ptions, **F**ont; select the size you want.
Change System colors	In the Help topic you want to change, select **O**ptions, **U**se System Colors; close Help and then restart Help.
Find Similar Topics	In the Find dialog box, type the word and click Find Si**m**ilar.

Applying Your Skills

1. Open Help using the keyboard. Look up how you would put a printer shortcut on your desktop from the Index tab and print out the Help topic.

2. In Help, find the topic about how to start Help, then annotate it to add the other shortcut methods you could use. Verify that there is a paper clip next to the Help topic title when you are through.

3. In the Help Contents tab, look up the best method available to you for troubleshooting if you have trouble using your network. Copy the text from the Help topic to your word processor.

4. In the Index tab in Help, look up topics that help you get more information on how to use the Paste Link command.

5. Change your Find tab settings so that Windows 95 searches all the words you type, in any order.

Project

5

Introduction to Networks

Objectives

In this project, you learn how to

➤ Find a Computer on a Network

➤ Browse Your Workgroup

➤ Share Folders, Files, and Printers on a Network

➤ Print and Troubleshoot Network Issues

➤ Connect to Remote Networks

➤ Connect to a Remote Machine Not Using Windows 95

Why Would I Do This?

f you work in a corporate environment, you most likely work on a networked system of computers connected in your company. Computers are networked to minimize the amount of system administration time that is necessary to maintain large numbers of computers in a busy office environment. Windows 95 enhances those features, allowing systems personnel to make changes to the entire network directly from their desktops instead of having to make personal visits to each help desk call that comes in.

How does this affect you? The network affects the way you access your computer, the way you access files and folders on your system, and the way you share information on your computer. If you had no network, you would turn on your computer and begin. Because of networks, you must type in your network ID and logon to identify to the network who is using the computer and what his or her preference settings are.

After you log on however, you have access to much more data, hardware, and software than you would be able to use without a network. This project introduces you to network dialog boxes you might encounter while getting around in a network. You also learn how to share information, print, and troubleshoot while working on a network. Throughout this project, your instructor will advise you about any instructions specific to your corporate system.

Lesson 1: Finding a Computer on a Network

In this lesson, you locate computers on the network. This provides a reference point from which you can begin a tour of your network. With Windows 95, you can double-click the Network Neighborhood icon to browse and use computers, printers, and data on your network and multiple networks. You can share a folder or printer with others. You can use the following steps to find the computers you will need.

If you have problems...

Network setups these days are as varied as department store aisles. Your company might be using Windows 95, Windows NT, Novell Netware, Banyan VINES, or a variety of other networks. Because of the large variety of configurations that can exist, this lesson might differ at points from your network.

While most steps remain universal, you might encounter differences between the configurations and steps described here, and those required by your company's network. If you have problems or run into such differences, ask your instructor for the procedure to use in your company. It is assumed in this project that you are working on a network; procedures for non-networked computers are not covered in this project. In addition, you can approach most networking steps from the Network Neighborhood, the Explorer, or My Computer. After completing this project, you can use whatever access method you prefer.

Lesson 1: Finding a Computer on a Network

If sharing is not enabled, you can turn it on by double-clicking the Network icon in the Control Panel. If you can't see a resource you're looking for, you might not have access permission.

To Find a Computer on a Network

❶ Open the Explorer.

You know from Project 1 that there are quite a few approaches you can take when opening Explorer. Refer to Project 1 if you need to refresh your memory on these steps.

❷ Right-click Network Neighborhood.

A new drop-down menu appears, which you have not previously seen (see Fig. 5.1). This menu is intuitive to the Network Neighborhood icon and offers options for that service.

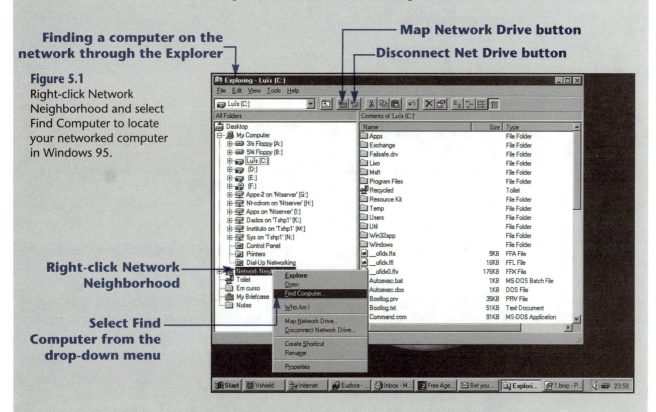

Finding a computer on the network through the Explorer

Figure 5.1
Right-click Network Neighborhood and select Find Computer to locate your networked computer in Windows 95.

Right-click Network Neighborhood

Select Find Computer from the drop-down menu

Map Network Drive button
Disconnect Net Drive button

❸ Click Find Computer.

This opens the Find Computer dialog box.

❹ Type the computer name provided by your instructor in the Named list box (see Fig. 5.2).

Your instructor will provide the name of the computer you should access. The computer's name might be something like Sales, IBDParis, or ntserver.

continues

102 Project 5 Introduction to Networks

To Find a Computer on a Network (continued)

Figure 5.2
The Find Computer dialog box quickly leads you to the computer you want to find.

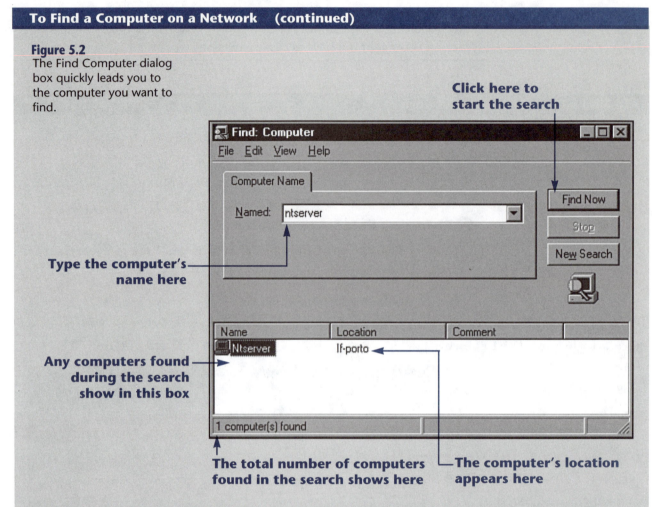

Click here to start the search

Type the computer's name here

Any computers found during the search show in this box

The total number of computers found in the search shows here

The computer's location appears here

5 **Click Find Now.**

Windows 95 searches the network for the computer you requested access to the same way it searches your hard disk for files or folders. Any matches to the search criteria appear at the bottom of the Find Computer dialog box. Location information and any comments provided are also visible in the search results area. If you want to work with that computer, double-click its information in your results window.

You can also start the process directly from the Start button to save time. Click Start, then choose **F**ind, **C**omputer. The Find Computer dialog box appears, just as it did in this lesson.

In the Find Computer dialog box, you can click Ne**w** Search to clear the current search box and begin again.

Lesson 2: Browsing Your Workgroup   **103**

Notice the arrow to the right of the **N**amed list box. Windows 95 saves recent searches to save you time when searching for computers.

Double-click the search results to instantly access the computer you were searching for.

Shared Folders
Shared folders are folders located on computers on a network that are shared or made available to more than one user.

You can also search for **shared folders** from the Find Computer dialog box. Just type the computer and folder path name. For example, you could type **legal\pleading\carson\january.doc**.

You don't always have to find a networked computer this way. After you locate a computer (or a folder, file, or printer), you can drag it to the Network Neighborhood folder. Then it will be available by double-clicking Network Neighborhood on your desktop.

6 Choose File, Close.

The Find Computer dialog box closes.

7 Click the Close button on the title bar in Explorer to close Explorer.

Lesson 2: Browsing Your Workgroup

In this project, you are becoming familiar with the Network Neighborhood you work in. You know how to locate a computer, but how can you find out how many printers or folders are available for you to use when you are on the network? This lesson shows you how to browse the network to see what items you have permission to access.

To Browse Your Workgroup

Network Neighborhood
Although the Network Neighborhood is an icon on your desktop, that icon represents a folder in your computer with the name Network Neighborhood, just as Word for Windows appears as a folder. If you use Explorer to access network items, it can provide a more comfortable interface for dealing with networked computers without limiting available features.

1 Double-click the Network Neighborhood icon on your desktop.

Network Neighborhood opens.

2 Right-click the Entire Network icon.

A drop-down menu appears, as shown in Figure 5.3. You can choose to **O**pen the Entire Network or **E**xplore it.

continues

To Browse Your Workgroup (continued)

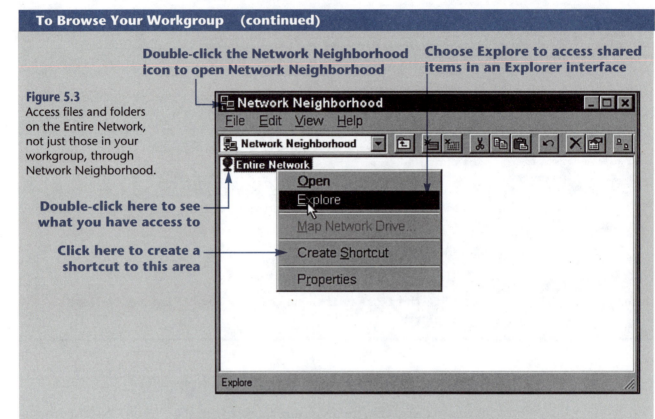

Figure 5.3
Access files and folders on the Entire Network, not just those in your workgroup, through Network Neighborhood.

3 Click Explore.

For this exercise and most exercises in this lesson, you use the familiar Explorer interface to browse your workgroup and entire network; in other words, your Network Neighborhood (see Fig. 5.4). When you feel comfortable with the concept of networks and shared resources, you might prefer to work in Network Neighborhood, or you might find it easier to stay in Explorer to find any items you need.

Lesson 2: Browsing Your Workgroup

Figure 5.4
The Explorer view of Network Neighborhood provides more information about items you are accessing than the information available when you use Network Neighborhood.

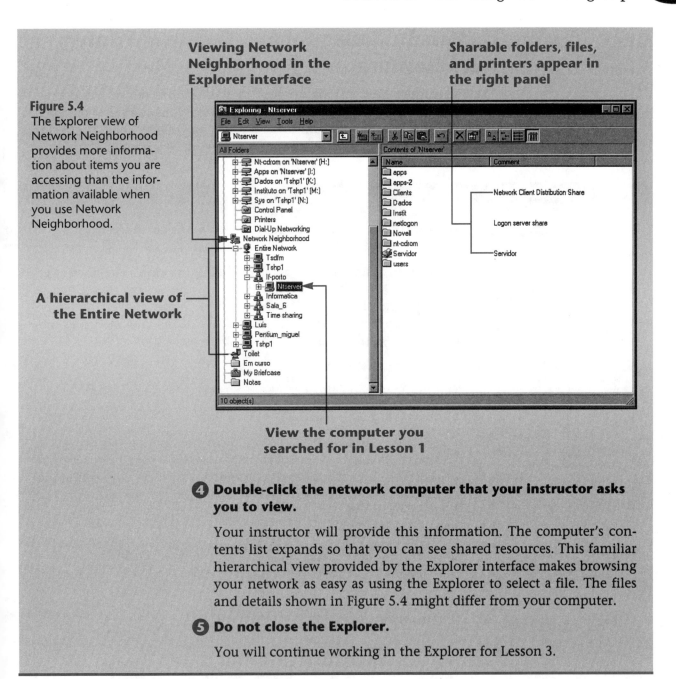

Viewing Network Neighborhood in the Explorer interface

Sharable folders, files, and printers appear in the right panel

A hierarchical view of the Entire Network

View the computer you searched for in Lesson 1

④ Double-click the network computer that your instructor asks you to view.

Your instructor will provide this information. The computer's contents list expands so that you can see shared resources. This familiar hierarchical view provided by the Explorer interface makes browsing your network as easy as using the Explorer to select a file. The files and details shown in Figure 5.4 might differ from your computer.

⑤ Do not close the Explorer.

You will continue working in the Explorer for Lesson 3.

You can search for any item in the Explorer that you have been given access rights to by your Systems Administrator.

You can create a shortcut to a network printer you use frequently. Browse for it either in Network Neighborhood or in the Explorer, then choose **F**ile, **I**nstall.

106 Project 5 Introduction to Networks

Lesson 3: Sharing Folders, Files, and Printers on a Network

You've learned how to look up your computer on a network and how to browse available printers, folders, and files from your computer on the network. In this lesson, you learn to set a folder so you can share it, open that shared file, use it, and add items to your Network Neighborhood folder.

To Share a Folder, File, or Printer

1 Locate the folder, file, or printer you want to share from the Explorer.

Ask your instructor for the name of the file or printer you are using in this step. Remember, all details of Network Servers are located in the right panel of the Explorer. In the Explorer, servers and their contents are displayed in the same way folders and their files are. Click to select the item you want to share.

2 Right-click the item.

The shortcut menu appears.

3 Click Sharing (see Fig. 5.5).

The Properties dialog box appears, with the Sharing tab displayed. This tab allows users to share the resources that have been set to be shared. You now can share this resource with users who can access it. The next steps show you how to open and use the resources you have access to.

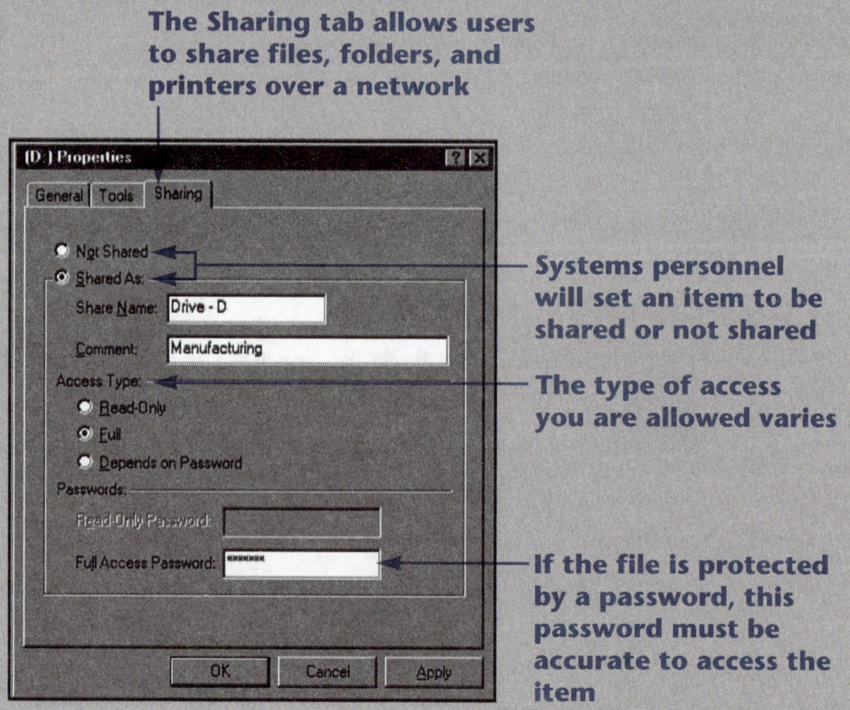

The Sharing tab allows users to share files, folders, and printers over a network

Figure 5.5
The Sharing tab, located in the Properties dialog box, allows items on the computer to be shared or not shared.

Systems personnel will set an item to be shared or not shared

The type of access you are allowed varies

If the file is protected by a password, this password must be accurate to access the item

Lesson 3 Sharing Folders, Files, and Printers on a Network   107

If you have problems...

If you do not see **S**haring as an option on the shortcut menu, the file might not be set for sharing. Ask your instructor which shared item to access, or see your Systems Administrator to have the folder settings changed. The item might be kept from sharing for security purposes.

The method used to add items to your Network Neighborhood is the same as copying and moving files in the Explorer using drag and drop. To add an item (files, folders, or printers) to your Network Neighborhood, right-click Start, choose **E**xplore, then double-click Entire Network.

Select the printer, folder, or file. Click in the right panel of the Explorer to select the item. Drag the item to the Network Neighborhood folder in the left panel. That item will now appear every time you open Network Neighborhood.

❹ Double-click the folder you want to open (see Fig. 5.6).

This opens the shared folder your instructor told you to open. In Windows 95, you no longer have to map a connection to a network drive, but you might want to under certain circumstances. You can still "map" a network drive to a shared networked item such as a folder. The next exercise explains how you can do this in Windows 95.

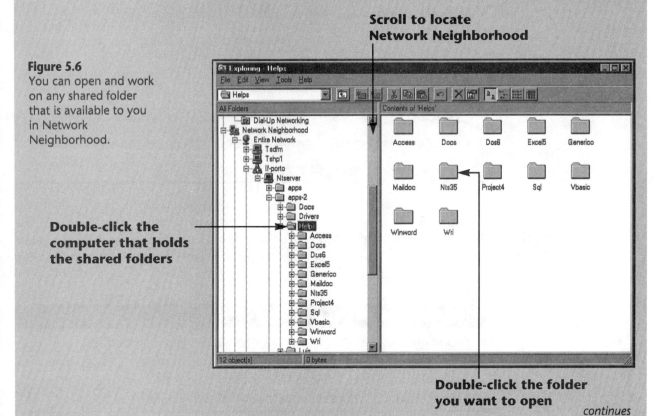

Figure 5.6
You can open and work on any shared folder that is available to you in Network Neighborhood.

continues

Project 5 Introduction to Networks

To Share a Folder, File, or Printer (continued)

5 **Click the Map Network Drive icon button on the toolbar in the Explorer, My Computer, or the Network Neighborhood.**

The Map Network Drive dialog box appears.

6 **From the D rive drop-down list, select the drive you want to search (see Figure 5.7).**

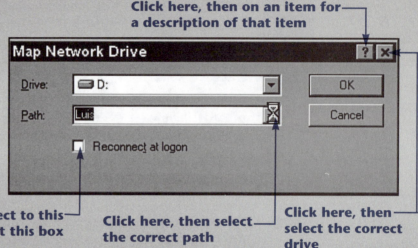

Figure 5.7
In Windows 95, it is not mandatory that you map a network drive. Click the Map Network Drive button if you need to need to use this feature.

Click here, then on an item for a description of that item

If you want to reconnect to this path at logon, select this box

Click here, then select the correct path

Click here, then select the correct drive

7 **In the P ath list box, enter the path (for example, \\computer-name\foldername).**

8 **Enter the password if your file is password-protected.**

You only need to enter a password if you are prompted to after entering the folder name. If Windows prompts you to enter a password, enter the password for that folder. This item is password-protected.

9 **Click OK.**

This action maps the drive and closes the Map Network Drive dialog box.

Windows 95 saves your mappings the same way it saves search words in the Find tab in your Help dialog box. After you map to a computer or folder, select the mapping you want to use again from the P ath drop-down list in the Map Network Drive dialog box.

If you have problems...

You might not see a toolbar in your Network Neighborhood, Explorer, or My Computer screen. To make a toolbar visible in most Microsoft applications, choose **V**iew, **T**oolbar. The toolbar will appear for you to access. Refer to Figure 5.1 to see the Map Network Drive button.

Lesson 4: Printing and Troubleshooting Network Issues

Lesson 4: Printing and Troubleshooting Network Issues

Printing from a shared printer in Windows 95 is very similar to printing from a printer that is attached directly to your computer. You can enjoy all the benefits of printing in Windows 95, including features such as using the Add Printer Wizard and viewing current items pending in the Printer Queue.

To Print a Document to a Network Printer

1 Open the Explorer.

2 Locate the computer that contains the printer you want to use.

Your instructor will tell you what printer to connect to. You can browse through the left panel of Explorer until you locate that computer.

3 Double-click the computer.

A new window appears, as shown in Figure 5.8.

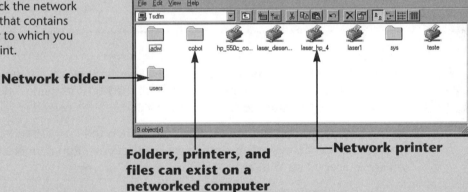

Figure 5.8
Double-click the network computer that contains the printer to which you want to print.

Network folder

Folders, printers, and files can exist on a networked computer

Network printer

If you don't know which computers have shared printers attached, choose **V**iew, **D**etails. You should be able to view printer names and comments in the Comment column.

4 Drag and drop the document from the right Explorer panel onto the printer icon.

The document prints. It probably won't be very long before you are going to need to see what items are pending in the printer queue. Sometimes you know you've sent a file to the printer, but nothing happens. The next step shows you how to check the status of the printer and see what items are waiting to be printed.

continues

110 Project 5 Introduction to Networks

> **To Print a Document to a Network Printer** (continued)
>
> **5** **Double-click the printer icon.**
>
> You can access this from Network Neighborhood, the Explorer, or My Computer. The printer folder opens displaying the jobs available in queue for that printer, as shown in Figure 5.9.
>
> **6** **View the current print jobs in queue.**
>
> You can view the document name, the current print status, and other information, such as the progress status of the print job.
>
>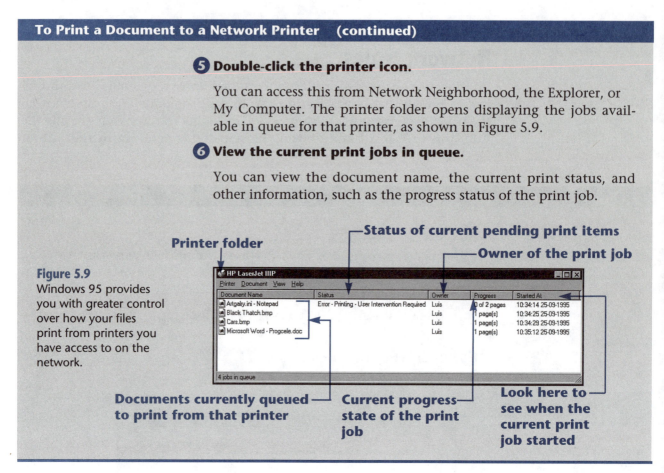
>
> **Figure 5.9**
> Windows 95 provides you with greater control over how your files print from printers you have access to on the network.

You learned how to use **R**un in Lesson 1 to save time when accessing items on your computer. You can also make good use of the **R**un command when trying to locate an item on a particular server when working in a networked environment.

Remember, you access Run by clicking Start. When the Run dialog box appears, type the server name (such as **ntserver** or **myserver**). Run connects you to the server. You might have to enter your password, if prompted.

The Explorer window opens. Select the printer you want to use. If you want to add a printer to another computer on the network, you can use the Add Printer Wizard, as covered in Project 3, Lesson 1, "Setting Up a Printer."

Lesson 5: Connecting to Remote Networks

In this project, you have focused on the network in your office. However, a big factor of networking in the current corporate world is mobile computing—connecting to your network outside the office.

In this lesson, you set up a connection to a remote computer, then connect to a remote network running Windows 95 and not running Windows 95 using Dial-Up Networking. The following exercises help to introduce you to this process. For companies not operating on the NT server platform, an additional step is necessary when configuring a connection to your network. Check with your System Administrator or instructor to verify which method you should use when connecting to the company network.

Lesson 5: Connecting to Remote Networks   111

When approaching this lesson on mobile computing, it is important to note that the upgrade process in any company is usually a gradual process on an as-needed basis. Many companies maintain legacy hardware. Newer technologies supported by Windows 95 include Plug and Play capability. Plug and Play is as it claims; you can plug an item such as a modem into the computer, or install a software application, and it runs without you having to know how to configure it or set it up.

Because it is likely that some form of legacy hardware or software will be used in your company, you might have to occasionally deal with legacy hardware or software issues.

Jargon Watch

Legacy hardware and software do not employ the new Plug and Play capability. Older hardware cannot interact as smoothly with a variety of interfaces as the newer Plug and Play hardware. Although Windows 95 is built to interact as smoothly as possible with legacy hardware, you cannot literally just plug the hardware in and have it function properly, which is possible with some Plug and Play hardware.

To Connect to a Remote Network

❶ Double-click My Computer on your desktop.

If you do not have a Dial-Up Networking icon in My Computer, it is not installed. Ask your System Administrator or instructor to install it so you can proceed.

❷ Double-click Dial-Up Networking.

The Dial-Up Networking window opens.

❸ Double-click Make New Connection to start the Make New Connection Wizard.

The Wizard appears and prompts you to answer questions that connect the computers (see Fig. 5.10).

Figure 5.10
Use the Make New Connection Wizard to connect to remote computers.

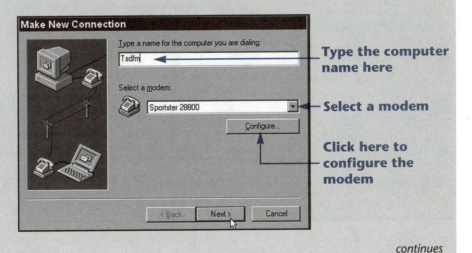

continues

Project 5 Introduction to Networks

To Connect to a Remote Network (continued)

To dial a connection you already set up, double-click its icon in the Dial-Up Networking window instead of the Make New Connection icon.

4 Type a name for the computer you are dialing.

You instructor will provide the computer name. Your instructions might differ slightly, such as the computer name or phone number you will dial. This dialog box also shows the attached modem type. You only need to configure this if you recently installed a new modem and it was not configured.

5 Click Next if you do not need to configure the modem type.

You move to the next wizard screen.

6 Verify that you are working in the correct connection.

You can click **B**ack at any time to change a setting.

7 Fill in any options that are not filled in.

Your instructor will walk you through the necessary steps to provide the needed information. All settings should be filled in before continuing your dial-up connection. Fill in the correct computer name for the computer you are dialing if it is not already available, as well as the modem type and phone number you are dialing. Portions might already be pre-configured by your system administrator.

8 Double-click Finish in the final wizard screen to connect to the computer at this time (see Fig. 5.11).

This information identifies the remote computer so that Windows can recognize when the correct computer has been located. Notice the new icon in your Dial-Up Networking window with the connection name you applied. This connection will remain available for future use.

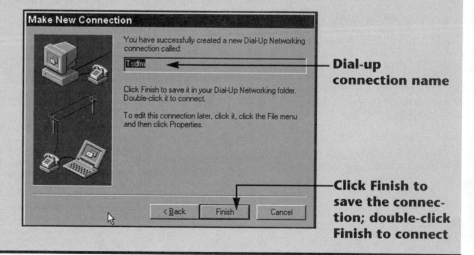

Figure 5.11
You can click Finish and save your new connection, or double-click to connect.

Lesson 6: Connecting to a Remote Machine Not Using Windows 95

 It's easy to create a shortcut to a network connection you use frequently. Press Ctrl+Shift while dragging the file to your desktop. Now you need only to double-click that icon to work with your files.

The preceding exercise works well if the remote PC runs Windows 95. But you might need to dial into a remote computer that uses another operating system. Suppose that you just finished setting up a connection to a remote computer, then the Systems Administrator tells you the remote machine runs on Novell Netware. You can re-open that dial-up information and change it so that Windows 95 can connect to the remote machine.

Lesson 6: Connecting to a Remote Machine Not Using Windows 95

Earlier, I discussed legacy hardware and software. Another legacy issue that will likely arise when using Dial-Up Networking is when you dial to connect to a remote machine. It is not using Windows 95, so it cannot handle the connection as intuitively as two computers using Windows 95 can. These steps allow you to access these computers.

To Connect to a Remote Machine Not Using Windows 95

1. Create your new connection as you did in "Connecting to a Remote Network," in Lesson 5.
2. Click once to select your new connection.
3. Choose File, Properties.

    The General tab of the My Connection dialog box appears.

4. Select Server Type.

    The Server Types dialog box appears, as shown in Figure 5.12. In this exercise, you only make changes to the type of dial-up server.

    continues

To Connect to a Remote Machine Not Using Windows 95 (continued)

Figure 5.12
The Server Types dialog box allows you to connect to a different operating system.

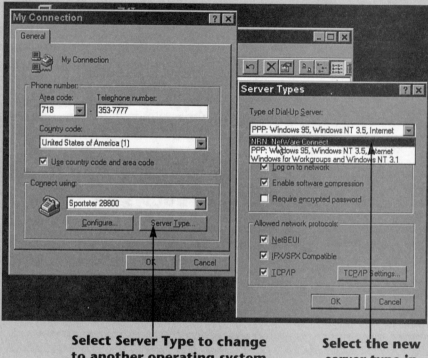

Select Server Type to change to another operating system

Select the new server type in the Server Types dialog box

⑤ Choose the type of server you are connecting to from the Type of Dial-Up Server drop-down list.

Your instructor has the correct server name for you to choose. You should not change any other settings in this box unless instructed to do so by your Systems Administrator.

⑥ Click OK.

Select OK again to close the My Connection dialog box.

Although you can change the server type, it is probably that you access computers not running Windows 95 through the feature called HyperTerminal. HyperTerminal is the recommended way to connect to computers not running Windows 95. You can also use HyperTerminal to send and receive files from such e-mail standards as CompuServe or MCI Mail.

Applying Your Skills   115

Project Summary

To	Do This
Find a computer on a network	Click Start, Find Computer; type the name; click Find Now.
Browse your workgroup	From Network Neighborhood, the Explorer, or My Computer, double-click the workgroup icon.
Share a network item	Right-click the item, click Sharing.
Open a network folder, file, or printer	Double-click the icon.
Map a Network Drive	From Network Neighborhood, the Explorer, or My Computer, click the Map Network drive icon; select the drive and path.
Print a document	Locate the document, drag the document to the printer icon.
View items in print queue	Double-click the printer icon.
Connect to a remote network	Use the Make New Connection Wizard unless you have a different operating system; use HyperTerminal for different operating systems.
Connect to a remote machine not using Windows 95	Create your new connection, choose File, Properties, select the General tab, click Server Type, select the correct server type.

Applying Your Skills

Finding Computers on a Network

1. Your instructor will give you a name of a computer.

2. Find the computer on your network using the Find command.

3. Open that computer from the results area.

4. Print the file to your default printer.

Browsing a Network

1. Find a printer in your workgroup. Your instructor will give you the printer name to use.

2. Print the same file to your workgroup printer.

3. Check the print queue to see the status of your request.

Connect to a Remote Network

1. Use the Make New Connection Wizard to connect to a remote network. Ask your instructor which network you should connect to.

2. Change the connection to a different network that uses a different operating system.

3. Rename the connection.

Project

6

Using the Briefcase

Objective

In this project, you learn how to

➤ Prepare Two Computers to Use the Briefcase

➤ Create a New Briefcase in Windows Explorer

➤ Copy Files to a New Briefcase In Explorer

➤ Return Briefcase Files to the Main Computer

➤ Use the Briefcase with Floppy Disks

Why Would I Do This?

With Windows 95, most office needs can be met. You can be productive—no matter where you are. You can work on office files from your home or portable computer, send and receive e-mail and faxes, forward documents in applications, even connect to CompuServe, the World Wide Web, and other online services. In this project, you learn how to use the Briefcase, a feature of Windows 95 that allows you to copy files to a new or current briefcase, work on files on your computer or a floppy disk when you are away from the office, synchronize files back onto your office computer, and print them.

After you master using the Briefcase, you can work on files, and communicate from any location with a computer and modem. You will most likely be using the Briefcase with a laptop computer provided by the company, so your instructor and Systems Administrator will provide you with the appropriate equipment to use during this project. The first thing you need to learn is how to connect two computers so that you can use the Briefcase.

Lesson 1: Preparing Two Computers to Use the Briefcase

Being able to leave the office, yet keep your productivity level high, is one of the benefits of the extended communications capabilities of Windows 95. The first thing you need to know is how to prepare your files to be worked on from a remote site. You might want to use the Briefcase feature to bring files home and work on them from a portable computer at home. Your home is then considered a remote site. With the Briefcase, you can transfer files from your desktop to your portable computer and work on them from anywhere.

It's easy to bring home files with the Briefcase. In the following exercise, you learn to how to connect two computers so you can transfer files back and forth. You might not have prior experience connecting two computers, but the Direct Cable Connection feature in Windows 95 makes it easy.

You need either a parallel or serial cable to connect the computers to each other. These should be available from your company, if the portable computer you will be using is provided by your company. Use Direct Cable Connection to assist you when connecting two computers. Direct Cable Connection is a wizard that walks you through the steps you need to take to connect two computers.

Lesson 1: Preparing Two Computers to Use the Briefcase

To Prepare Two Computers to Use the Briefcase

1 **Click Start and choose Programs, Accessories, Direct Cable Connection.**

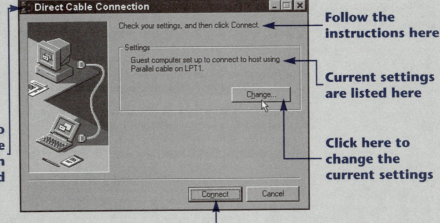

Figure 6.1
Direct Cable Connection connects two computers so that they can share files without a network.

Connect two computers using the Direct Cable Connection Wizard

Follow the instructions here

Current settings are listed here

Click here to change the current settings

Click here to begin the connecting process

Direct Cable Connection helps you connect two computers with a cable. The Direct Cable Connection Wizard appears (see Figure 6.1) and walks you through the steps necessary to configure your computer. The Wizard acts as a guide to ask you the appropriate questions and set the options you request, as you set your connection.

2 **Check the settings listed as your current settings in the Direct Cable Connection Wizard.**

You will be prompted to check your settings.

3 **Check with your instructor or Systems Administrator to determine whether your system's settings are correct.**

You might find that your configuration is correct. If your connection is set correctly, then you can ignore the rest of the steps in this lesson. Click Connect rather than Change, if your current settings are correct. If you need to change the current settings, proceed to step 4.

4 **Click Change if you need to make changes to the current settings.**

The Direct Cable Connection Wizard screen changes and prompts you for more information about the computer you are using (see Fig. 6.2).

continues

Project 6 Using the Briefcase

To Prepare Two Computers to Use the Briefcase (continued)

Figure 6.2
You can use a host or guest computer to make a Direct Cable Connection.

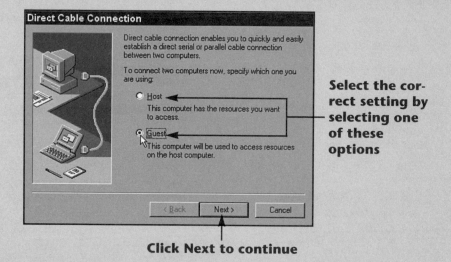

Select the correct setting by selecting one of these options

Click Next to continue

5 **Select the correct button. Your instructor will tell you whether the computer you are using is a host or a guest computer.**

The **host** is the computer that has the resources you need to reach. The **guest** is the computer you will use to access the information. The default is set to guest. In most cases, you will accept this default, but be sure to ask your instructor.

6 **Click Next to move to the next Wizard screen.**

Select the port you will use, either parallel or serial (see Fig. 6.3). This will match the type of cable you will be using. Use a parallel cable to connect between parallel ports; use a serial cable to connect between serial ports.

Figure 6.3
You can use either a parallel or serial cable to connect two computers.

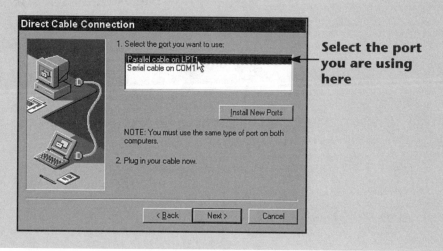

Select the port you are using here

Lesson 1: Preparing Two Computers to Use the Briefcase

7 **Insert the cable to connect the two computers now. Click Next to move to the next screen. The Wizard tells you that you have successfully completed your connection.**

The Wizard reminds you that you must install your Direct Cable Connection on both computers. Please ask your instructor or System Administrator to verify that the other computer you will use has been properly set up for Direct Cable Connection. If it hasn't, configure that computer with the guidance of your instructor at this time.

8 **Click Finish, and your connection initializes.**

A screen appears to indicate that the connection is enabling, as shown in Figure 6.4.

Figure 6.4
The Direct Cable Connection displays the status of the connection.

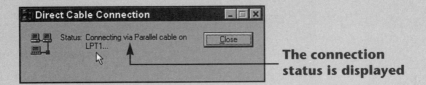

The connection status is displayed

9 **Click Close.**

You have now set up the current computer connection.

Jargon Watch

For users familiar with earlier versions of Windows, several new terms are used in Windows 95.

Direct Cable Connection allows a portable computer to access files on a desktop computer by connecting the two computers with a cable. If the desktop computer happens to be on a network, you also can access network files and folders.

The **Briefcase** is a tool in Windows 95 that appears as an icon on your desktop. Use the Briefcase to move and synchronize files and folders between computers.

Dial-Up Networking is a tool you use to dial into your corporate network when working from home or on the road. Dial-Up Networking was also used in Project 5 to dial directly into the office without using the Briefcase.

The **World Wide Web** is a collection of online sites and services covering an expansive array of topics.

A **parallel cable** or **serial cable** attaches two computers through a parallel or serial port on the computers. A parallel or serial **port** is the jack in the computer where you plug in the cable; the port provides the connection point between cable and computer.

Lesson 2: Creating a New Briefcase in the Explorer

You now know how to connect two computers if you need to copy files from your computer to a laptop or floppy disk. You might notice a Briefcase already located on your desktop. If you do, your Systems Administrator has created that for you to use. However, you will probably not find a Briefcase available to use when you begin working with the Briefcase. In this lesson, you learn how to create a new Briefcase so that you can copy files to it.

You have been working in the Explorer in most of your previous lessons, as well as when you set up your Direct Cable Connection. You will continue to work in the Explorer for this lesson.

To Create a New Briefcase In the Explorer

❶ Open the Explorer.

You can create a new Briefcase in Windows Explorer (see Fig. 6.5).

❷ Choose View, Details for browsing in this lesson.

Use the button on the far right end of the Explorer toolbar to view file details.

Figure 6.5
If your Briefcase is not visible on the Desktop, locate it from inside Windows Explorer.

Use the File menu to create a new Briefcase

You can access available Briefcases in the Explorer

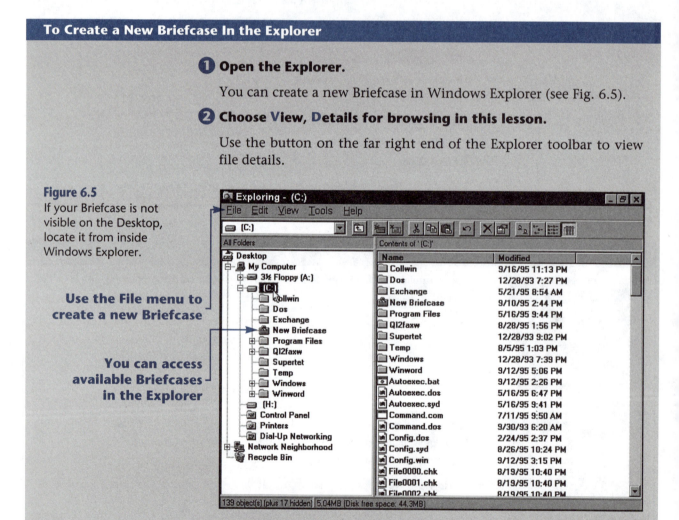

If you have problems...

You should be able to see the status bar at the bottom of the Explorer screen. The status bar keeps you informed about procedures being performed, the amount of free disk space available, the size of current contents. It also describes buttons when you pause over them. If it is not visible, choose **V**iew, Status **B**ar.

Lesson 2: Creating a New Briefcase in the Explorer   123

3 Select File, New.

There are many options available when you choose New. Table 6.1 describes these options in detail.

4 Select Briefcase from the menu (see Figure 6.6).

Figure 6.6
You can accomplish complex file synchronizations between computers through the easy steps available in the Briefcase feature.

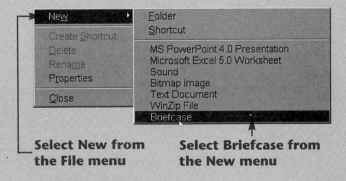

Select New from the File menu

Select Briefcase from the New menu

Office 95
Office 95 is a collection of applications designed to work seamlessly with Windows 95. Applications can include Word for Windows, Excel, PowerPoint, Access, and Scheduler.

You might see different options on your computer from those listed in Table 6.1. For example, you might already work in an Office 95 environment. In that case, your application references will indicate newer versions.

5 Release the mouse button to create the new briefcase.

The new briefcase is available and selected so that you can easily rename it (see Fig. 6.7).

Figure 6.7
Rename the new Briefcase.

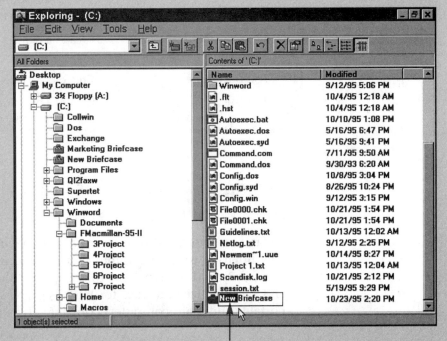

The new Briefcase appears in the right panel of the Explorer

continues

124 Project 6 Using the Briefcase

To Create a New Briefcase In the Explorer (continued)

6 Type New Briefcase in the selected area and press ⏎Enter.

The new Briefcase icon appears selected in the right panel of the Explorer. The new Briefcase title is now the name you typed. Keep Explorer open for the next lesson.

Table 6.1 describes the options available in the File, New submenu.

Table 6.1 New Items that Can Be Created from the File Menu in Explorer	
Option	**Function**
Folder	Creates a new folder to organize and hold files of a similar nature.
Shortcut	Creates a shortcut for the selected file directly on your desktop.
PowerPoint 4.0 Presentation	Creates a PowerPoint document. This file extension is PPT.
Excel 5.0 Worksheet	Creates a document in Excel 5.0. This file extension is XLS.
Word 6.0 Document	Creates a Word 6.0 document. This file extension is DOC.
Sound	Creates a sound file. This file extension is WAV.
Bitmap Image	Creates a bitmap, or graphics file. This file extension is BMP.
Text Document	Creates a text file. This file extension is TXT.
Briefcase	Creates a new Briefcase to use when synchronizing files between computers.

Lesson 3: Copying Files to a New Briefcase in the Explorer

So far, you've learned how to connect two computers. You've also created a new Briefcase to hold the files you need to work on away from the office. Now, you need to learn how to set up the Briefcase so that you can transfer and synchronize your files for later use. You should currently still have the portable and main computers connected by either a parallel or serial cable.

Lesson 3: Copying Files to a New Briefcase in the Explorer 125

To Copy Files to a New Briefcase in the Explorer

❶ Browse to select the files or folders your instructor advises you to work with.

You can select contiguous files by selecting the first file, scrolling to the last file you need, pressing ⇧Shift, and clicking the last file. If your files are non-contiguous, press Ctrl each time you click to select another file.

❷ Drag the files you selected on top of the correct Briefcase icon.

Be careful to place the item or items that you are dragging directly onto the correct icon. In this case, you will not need to press and hold the Ctrl button when dragging the files. Because you are working in the Briefcase, the system knows to maintain the original file.

❸ Release the mouse button when your mouse is located directly over your new Briefcase.

The Briefcase icon will appear to be selected. A message box appears briefly to check and update your files. You can click the Cancel button at this time if you want to undo your selection.

❹ Click your Briefcase icon in the left panel of the Explorer to view exactly what items are in the Briefcase in the right panel (see Fig. 6.8).

After you copy the files to your Briefcase, you can work on either version of the file, portable or main, without losing proper synchronization.

Figure 6.8
The contents of the current Briefcase display in the right panel, listing which file the Briefcase icon is to synchronize with and the status of other data.

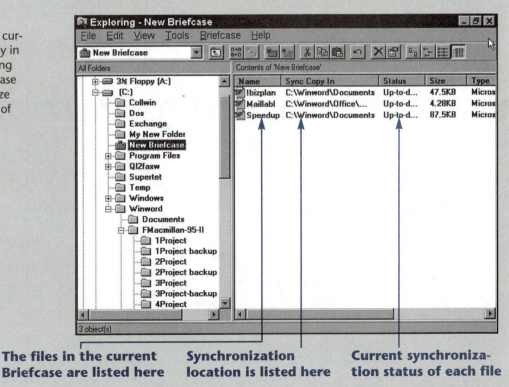

The files in the current Briefcase are listed here

Synchronization location is listed here

Current synchronization status of each file

continues

126 Project 6 Using the Briefcase

To Learn Parts of the Screen (continued)

5 **Select the new Briefcase icon.**

Do not select the individual folders in the Briefcase. Select the Briefcase itself in the left panel.

6 **Press** Ctrl **and drag the Briefcase to your desktop.**

This makes the Briefcase readily visible for you to use.

7 **Close the Explorer on your computer.**

The Briefcase icon will be on your desktop.

If you have problems...

You don't need to be concerned about copying over a file already located in the Briefcase. If you try to copy a file already located in the Briefcase, a sign appears, indicating file information and asking you to verify that you want to copy over the file currently in Briefcase.

Lesson 4: Returning Briefcase Files to the Main Computer

After you create your connection and Briefcase, copy your files, and make the necessary changes, you need to know how to synchronize your files back onto your company computer. Your instructor has advised you to edit the file you copied to your Briefcase so that you can see the changes that take place when you synchronize the initial file with the edited file. Follow these steps to synchronize your file or files.

To Return Briefcase Files to the Main Computer

1 **Right-click Start.**

You should open both the Explorer and the Briefcase to return the synchronized files to their original location. This lets you verify the synchronization process. If you want to update all and don't want to view the transfer, you can select **U**pdate All from the Briefcase icon without opening it. But for this exercise, you will copy only one edited file back to the desktop.

2 **Click E**xplore.

The Explorer opens.

3 **Double-click the Briefcase icon.**

The Briefcase icon is located on your desktop from the earlier exercise.

Lesson 5: Using the Briefcase with Floppy Disks 127

4 Reconnect the two computers.

You can do this with a cable. If you have a Plug-and-Play-compliant machine, you can just pop the laptop into your desktop computer to return the updated files to the main computer. In this case, you do not need the cable to connect the two computers.

5 Verify that both computers are on.

The Briefcase will not transfer files if both computers are not on.

6 Select one file in your current Briefcase screen.

If you want to synchronize all files in the Briefcase, choose Update All from the Briefcase menu. You will only update the file you selected in this exercise. You can update individual files using Update Selection. The files are automatically updated and synchronized on the main computer, as directed.

7 View the update screen.

This screen appears, showing the status of the transfer and synchronization (see Fig. 6.9).

Figure 6.9
The Briefcase provides a screen to show the transfer status.

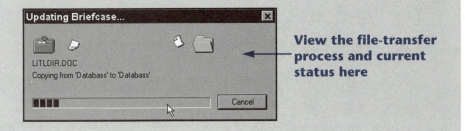

View the file-transfer process and current status here

Lesson 5: Using the Briefcase with Floppy Disks

You may not always be able to use a cable to synchronize files between two computers. But you still want the synchronization feature offered by the Briefcase in Windows 95. In this lesson, you learn how to copy files to the Briefcase on a floppy disk. You can then use the floppy disk version of the Briefcase to work on files. You need a floppy disk that is compatible with your disk drive for this lesson.

To Use the Briefcase with a Floppy Disk

1 Insert a floppy disk in the disk drive on the main computer.

In most cases, your disk drive will be compatible with 3 1/2-inch floppy disks.

2 Open the Windows Explorer.

Place the Explorer in a location on your desktop that allows you to work between the Explorer and the Briefcase.

continues

To Use the Briefcase with a Floppy Disk   (continued)

3 **Select any files you will be working with when you are away from the office.**

You can also copy a shortcut to your Briefcase if you want.

4 **Copy the files or folders to the Briefcase icon.**

Use drag and drop to copy the files (see Figure 6.10).

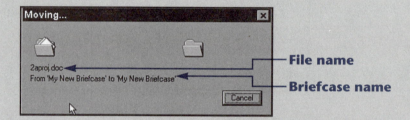

Figure 6.10
A screen appears, indicating what file and briefcase are being copied.

5 **Copy the Briefcase to the floppy disk.**

Copy these files by dragging the Briefcase icon (either on your desktop or in Explorer) over drive A:.

6 **Exit Windows 95, and disconnect the computers.**

If you are using Plug-and-Play-compliant hardware, you don't need to shut down the operating system to disconnect the systems. Your Systems Administrator can tell you if you are using Plug-and-Play equipment.

7 **Start your operating system on your portable computer or home computer.**

Because you are working with a floppy disk, you have more flexibility to choose the equipment you want to work on.

8 **Insert your floppy disk into the disk drive on your portable or home computer.**

You can work directly from the disk when using the Briefcase.

You can edit files more quickly by working directly on your portable computer, rather than working from the disk. To do this in the Explorer, drag the Briefcase to the portable desktop to work. When you finish editing, copy it back to the disk.

9 **Open the Windows Explorer on your home computer.**

You can also use My Computer to access the Briefcase. Just remember, you save system resources by using the Windows Explorer.

10 **Double-click the Briefcase icon to see and edit the files in Briefcase.**

When you finish editing files or folders, save the files as usual, and return the floppy disk to your main computer. The rest of the steps

Project Summary

in this lesson explain how to synchronize and print the Briefcase files from a floppy disk.

⑪ Right-click the Briefcase icon after you insert your floppy disk into your office computer (see Figure 6.11).

⑫ This opens the shortcut menu. Choose U̲pdate All in the Briefcase shortcut menu. If you do not want to update all your files or folders, you can open the Briefcase, select only the files you want to update, and click U̲pdate Selection from the Briefcase menu.

Figure 6.11
You don't have to open the Briefcase to synchronize all files back to the desktop.

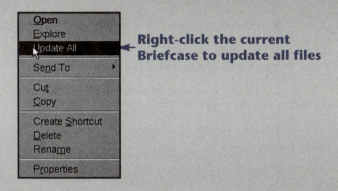

 If your computer is not currently attached to a printer, you can still send files to the print queue. You usually do this in the application, from the F̲ile menu. However, this can vary between products. Windows 95 automatically stores the print requests with the Briefcase files or folders. Windows 95 automatically prints those files held in the print queue. It is not necessary to take any steps to initiate printing.

Project Summary

To	Do This
Connect two computers	Connect via cable, choose Start, P̲rograms, Accessories, Direct Cable Connection; follow the Wizard instructions.
Create a new Briefcase	Right-click Start, E̲xplore, F̲ile, Ne̲w, F̲older; name the folder; press ⏎Enter.
Copy files to a Briefcase	Drag and drop selected files to the Briefcase icon.
Update all files	Double-click the Briefcase; choose B̲riefcase, Update All.
Update selected files	Open the Briefcase; select the files; choose B̲riefcase, U̲pdate Selection.
To work with floppies	Copy the Briefcase to a disk; edit the files as needed; copy the Briefcase back to desktop; choose to update a single file or all files.

Applying Your Skills

Create a New Briefcase

1. Set up a new Briefcase on your desktop.

2. Create two new files in your word processing package as in step 3.

3. Create a file with your instructor's name in the body, and name it INSTFILE.DOC. Create a file with your name in the body, and name it BRFILE.DOC.

4. Find both files in the Explorer. Copy them to the Briefcase.

Prepare a Briefcase to Use

1. Connect two computers, and move the new Briefcase to the portable computer or floppy disk.

2. Edit the file by adding your name to the file body (either on the main computer or the portable).

3. Reconnect the computers and update each file individually, not all at once.

Accessing The Microsoft Network

Objective

In this project, you learn how to
- ➤ Access The Microsoft Network and See What It Offers
- ➤ Navigate Categories and Member Assistance
- ➤ Browse for Information
- ➤ Download a File from The Microsoft Network
- ➤ Access and Use Chat Rooms
- ➤ Sign Out of The Microsoft Network

Why Would I Want To Do This?

The Microsoft Network (MSN) is an essential underlying component of the features you have learned in this book. E-mail and faxing are two important services you have used that utilize The Microsoft Network. In this project, you learn about more features that The Microsoft Network gives you.

Because of Windows 95's multitasking capability, you can simultaneously download an application, send and receive e-mail, check postings on a bulletin board service, and order travel tickets, all in a familiar Windows 95 interface. The Microsoft Network provides worldwide access to bulletin boards, chat rooms, file libraries, and e-mail, along with expert technical assistance, such as the Microsoft Most Frequently Asked Questions. In this project, you learn about The Microsoft Network and the Internet, how to use them to your benefit (both at work and away from the office), and how to find what you want in The Microsoft Network.

Although most people currently think of online service providers as entertainment, most businesses today know that the Internet, the World Wide Web, and online providers are mandatory factors in the future of systems planning. The Microsoft Network provides the tools to deal with a global business environment directly from your operating system, Windows 95. In Lesson 1, you access The Microsoft Network.

Jargon Watch

The whole concept of the online environment is foreign to many people. Throughout this project, terms will be defined and graphic examples provided so you become comfortable while you work in The Microsoft Network.

Windows 95's **multitasking** capabilities allow you to perform more than one task simultaneously. You are limited only by the amount of RAM, or memory, available in your computer. Each application is considered separately in Windows 95.

The **Internet** is a loosely organized worldwide group of networks that has been in existence for over 20 years. The networks consist of government, education, and corporate computers. A massive number of resources exist to aid you in gathering information.

Online service providers, such as America Online, Prodigy, CompuServe, The Microsoft Network, and Internet service providers offer access to the Internet and other commercial offerings for a fee. These services can provide an easier graphical interface to the Internet for the novice user rather than character-based interfaces.

Downloading a file simply means retrieving a file from a file library on an online service and copying it to your computer's hard disk—to make the file available for your use. You might want to download an application that helps you compress files, the latest menu from an exclusive restaurant your client wants to visit, or an upgrade to The Microsoft Network. You can view the cost of downloading a file (many are free) and the file content, then decide if you want to download that file. In The Microsoft Network, you can do this by double-clicking an icon.

Lesson 1: Accessing MSN and Seeing What It Offers   133

The World Wide Web is known as the graphical portion of the Internet and can be accessed through MSN only with Microsoft Plus! (which does not come in the standard Windows 95 operating system). Web access is considered an add-on, or feature enhancer, to Windows 95. The World Wide Web provides an enormous array of information and facts available for the user. Users can browse information or products that are of interest to them, receive information, or place an order.

Lesson 1: Accessing MSN and Seeing What It Offers

You'll be surprised how easy it is to connect to MSN. The Microsoft Network should already be set up on your computer by your System Administrator or instructor. You might already be registered for MSN, or your company might leave this process to you. In this lesson, you learn how to sign up and access MSN. You also familiarize yourself with the initial screen you see when you access MSN.

To Sign Up and Access The Microsoft Network

1 **Double-click the MSN icon located on your computer desktop.**

The Sign In dialog box appears, as shown in Figure 7.1. However, if you have not yet registered, you will see a three step Sign-Up dialog box instead. You need to enter information such as your name, phone number, and credit card number if you see this box. After you sign up, you can proceed to step 2.

Figure 7.1
If you are already registered with The Microsoft Network, the Sign In dialog box will be the first window you see when logging on.

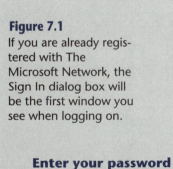

Enter your password here

Click this box and MSN will remember your password for you

Choose Connect to continue to MSN Central

Choose Cancel to exit The Microsoft Network

Sign in by typing your Member ID here

Click Settings to change connection settings

continues

To Sign Up and Access The Microsoft Network   (continued)

❷ Type your member ID and Password in the appropriate text boxes.

This password is your Microsoft Network Password. Your member ID will most likely be the name set up by the System Administrator in your company. Check with your System Administrator or instructor if you do not know this information.

❸ Make sure the Remember My Password check box has a check in it. If it doesn't, click it once to select it.

This allows you to log on in the future without typing your password each time.

❹ Click Connect to initiate the connection to The Microsoft Network.

You might need to change settings, such as the access number, dialing properties, or modem settings, as shown in Figure 7.2. This might occur if you are accessing MSN from a portable computer, for example, in a location other than your office. If you think you need to check or change any of your system settings, click the Settings button in the Sign In dialog box to access the dialog box where you can change this information. Details on how to work with your settings are provided later in this project.

Figure 7.2
The Connection Settings dialog box allows you to reconfigure your connection to The Microsoft Network.

If you want to use a different access number to dial in, click here

Change call-in settings (such as calling card) here

Adjust the modem setting here

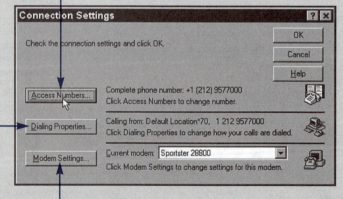

Two windows might pop up simultaneously, MSN Central and MSN Today. MSN Central is the base from which all MSN options appear (see Fig. 7.3). MSN Today pops up to notify you of the special topics of interest for the day (see Figure 7.4).

MSN Central is the main Microsoft Network window that appears immediately after you sign in. From here you can go to

▶ MSN Today

▶ E-mail

Lesson 1: Accessing MSN and Seeing What It Offers   135

- Favorite Places
- Member Assistance
- Categories

See Table 7.1 at the end of this lesson for more information about each area of The Microsoft Network.

Figure 7.3
MSN Central's main access window provides a number of ways to access the information you want: you can click on a bar or access items through the Edit menu.

Holds icons to locations you prefer

Click here to access the category tree in all categories

Click here to find out the latest news and current events

Receive help for new members and current users

MSN Central   Click once to enter an area

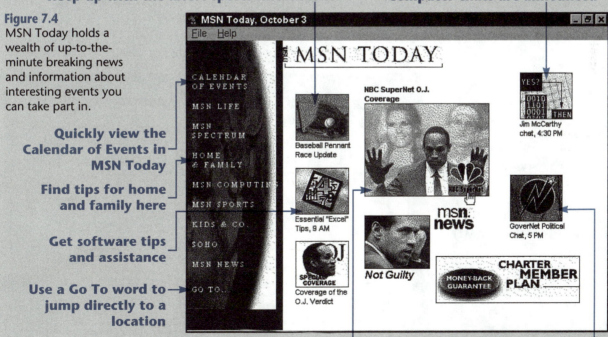

Keep up with the latest sports information   Computer chats are announced

Figure 7.4
MSN Today holds a wealth of up-to-the-minute breaking news and information about interesting events you can take part in.

Quickly view the Calendar of Events in MSN Today

Find tips for home and family here

Get software tips and assistance

Use a Go To word to jump directly to a location

Important news coverage is provided through MSN Today

Chats for all topics are announced and available here

continues

Project 7 Accessing The Microsoft Network

To Sign Up and Access The Microsoft Network (continued)

❺ Click any picture on the MSN Today window.

For example, if you click the Essential Excel Tips picture, a secondary window might appear, inviting you to join in a chat by an author specializing in Excel and offering tips. It would tell you when the chat is going to begin and where you can go to participate. You can also click the text in the left panel for information regarding certain topics.

❻ Click the Close button on the title bar to close MSN Today.

The MSN Today screen closes, and you are once again in the MSN Central screen.

❼ Click the E-mail button to open Microsoft Exchange and your Inbox.

You can adjust settings so that your mail automatically downloads when you log on to The Microsoft Network. You will be notified when new mail arrives.

❽ Click the Favorite Places button in MSN Central to access Favorite Places.

The Favorite Places window opens, as shown in Figure 7.5. Everyone has different interests, business orientations, and hobbies. You might, for example, need to keep up with emerging computer technologies for lending capital, while other people in your company do not need this information. You can put shortcuts to these items in your Favorite Places folder. Here you have a concise listing of only those areas of MSN that suit your interest.

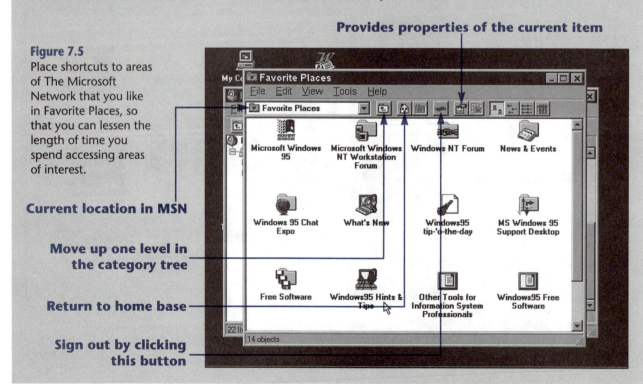

Figure 7.5
Place shortcuts to areas of The Microsoft Network that you like in Favorite Places, so that you can lessen the length of time you spend accessing areas of interest.

Provides properties of the current item

Current location in MSN

Move up one level in the category tree

Return to home base

Sign out by clicking this button

Lesson 1: Accessing MSN and Seeing What It Offers 137

⑨ Click the Up One Level button to move back to MSN Central.

If the toolbar is not visible in the Favorite Places window, choose **V**iew, **T**oolbar. Categories and Member Assistance both provide topical information. Because Member Assistance is information about members, it is discussed in the Categories section.

⑩ Leave The Microsoft Network window open.

You will continue to leave MSN open throughout this project, so that you will not have to log on repeatedly, so keep MSN open at the end of each lesson in this project until the project is completed and you are instructed to log out of MSN.

Another way to open The Microsoft Network is through the Start menu. Click Start, choose **P**rograms, then select The Microsoft Network. This opens MSN in Windows Explorer view, a two-panel screen in which the category is listed in the left panel and the subcategories are shown in the right panel.

You can also right-click the MSN icon on your desktop and choose **E**xplore for the Explorer interface, or **O**pen for the standard MSN interface.

For this project, you will be using both views provided to familiarize you with your options.

You can deselect this check box to provide an extra level of logon protection. Because there is a fee for connection time to The Microsoft Network, leaving this box blank will prevent other users from being able to access MSN if you are away from your computer for an extended period of time.

If the MSN Today window did not automatically appear, you can activate it by clicking the MSN Today bar once in the MSN Central window. Clicking the picture activates further information about the topic.

If MSN Today pops up automatically and you do not want it to, choose **T**ools, **O**ptions in MSN Central and deselect the box for MSN Today. Return to the MSN Central window.

You can send and receive mail with individuals over the Internet. You need to know their e-mail addresses, such as `rneilson@hooked.net`. People who send you Internet mail need to address mail to your address, which is `memberID@msn.com`. It will arrive in your Inbox in Microsoft Exchange.

138 Project 7 Accessing The Microsoft Network

Table 7.1	MSN Central Elements
Feature	Description
MSN Today	Updates you about current events, what is going on in MSN, special forums and chats, announcements, and opportunities.
E-mail	You can access your e-mail in MSN with a single click on this button.
Favorite Places	Everyone will have different preferences about what interests them in MSN. If you like an area and want to be able to return to it again quickly and easily, store it in your Favorite Places folder.
Member Assistance	You can find an answer or place an inquiry about any help you might need in MSN. Whether you are new to MSN, have a billing question, or want to find out where to go to get information, this is the location for assistance.
Categories	A vast assortment of categories, titles, and options are available in a category tree. Browse the Categories to familiarize yourself with MSN and locate your own favorite places to visit. You can create a desktop shortcut to any place you want.

Lesson 2: Navigating Categories and Member Assistance

Member Assistance is an easy-to-use area where you can learn about MSN, master the rules for operating in the MSN environment, see how to fit in with the language used, get answers to your questions, make a posting to a bulletin board service, and even get some practice before actually going online in a chat room. In this lesson, you learn how to get around in MSN's Member Assistance area.

Categories contains access to an abundance of information, chat rooms, bulletin board services, companies, and other interesting features.

To Navigate Categories and Member Assistance

1 Right-click the Member Assistance button in MSN Central and select Explore to access all member information in the familiar Explorer interface.

The Member Assistance window opens, as shown in Figure 7.6.

Lesson 2: Navigating Categories and Member Assistance   139

Figure 7.6
If you aren't yet comfortable with how to move around in MSN, visit the Member Assistance window for friendly help and answers to your questions.

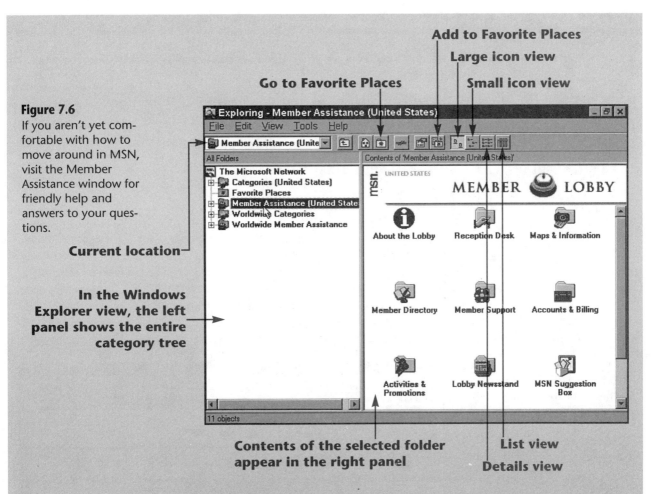

2. **Double-click the About the Lobby icon to see further information about the Member Assistance area. Refer to this area if you have any questions when you are on your own later in The Microsoft Network.**

3. **Return to MSN Central.**

   You can do this by clicking the Go to MSN Central button on the toolbar; or by choosing Edit, Go to, MSN Central; or by clicking the Up One Folder button on the toolbar.

4. **Click the Categories button in MSN Central to access the category tree on MSN.**

   The Categories listing appears and displays the category options available. You might see a different view than the figures listed in this book. The Microsoft Network offers several view types, so you can find one that is comfortable for you. The four view types provided are Large icons, Small icons, Details, and List. You can change views, just as you can anywhere in Windows 95, by using the icons located on the right side of the toolbar (refer to Fig. 7.6).

   continues

140 Project 7 Accessing The Microsoft Network

To Navigate Categories and Member Assistance (continued)

❺ Click each icon as your instructor describes each view to you.

Although the views are similar, you should use the view your instructor advises during these exercises. When you are through with this exercise, set MSN to the view you prefer to use by default.

❻ Right-click the Business and Finance folder.

A shortcut menu appears (see Fig. 7.7).

❼ Choose Explore.

The Business and Finance folder has further options. Do not perform this step if you are already in Explorer view. In Explorer view, you see the plus (+) sign/minus (–) sign box to the left of the category tree, like Windows Explorer, and you can view much more information at a glance than if you use the default view. In this view, click to expand or collapse your view of options available.

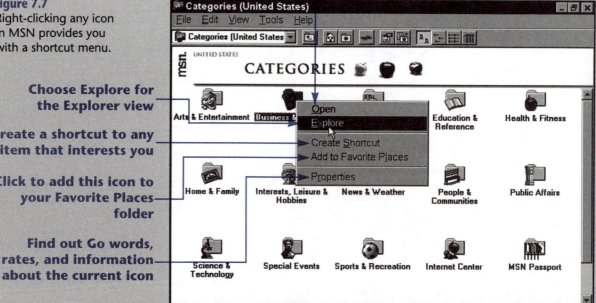

Figure 7.7
Right-clicking any icon in MSN provides you with a shortcut menu.

Click here to open the item selected

Choose Explore for the Explorer view

Create a shortcut to any item that interests you

Click to add this icon to your Favorite Places folder

Find out Go words, rates, and information about the current icon

❽ Click the Professions & Industries icon.

Use whatever method you prefer to open the Professions & Industries folder, and examine the contents.

❾ Right-click Professions & Industries, and select Add to Favorite Places. Professions & Industries will now be available the next time you access your Favorite Places.

⑩ Click the Favorite Places icon on the toolbar.

You see the Professions & Industries icon located in Favorite Places. You should currently be working in the MSN default of a separate window opening each time you click. Close all but MSN Central.

⑪ Click to select the MSN Central window.

You need to be in MSN Central to begin your next lesson. Remember, if you find an icon that interests you, add it to your Favorite Places folder so you can easily find it later. (This will also help to keep costs down by providing a clear path directly to your title of interest.)

The offerings in The Microsoft Network can seem limitless. You might use an icon so frequently you want it even handier than the Favorite Places folder. Create a shortcut directly to your desktop. Simply drag the icon to your desktop if it is visible. Windows tells you that the shortcut was successfully created. If you can't see the desktop, you can right-click the icon and select Create **S**hortcut.

Lesson 3: Downloading a File from MSN

In Lessons 1 and 2, you accessed MSN and saw an array of options containing interesting information. You learned how to access windows to view choices available to you. You might have noticed files available in The Microsoft Network, but you want to know how to retrieve the files you see, or download an interesting file, such as a utility that compresses documents.

The capability to download files from a file library in The Microsoft Network is crucial. It provides a way to find business solutions not available to the user of a stand-alone computer. As an example, if your modem does not function properly because you have an older modem that is not compatible with Windows 95, you might be able to download an updated driver that allows you to successfully install and configure your modem and begin using it right away. Without this capability, your modem would be useless until the manufacturer could send you a copy of the updated driver file. In this lesson, you learn how to recognize a file available for your use, and how to download that file when you need it.

Some areas of MSN charge a fee for downloading or copying files. For example, a software application might be available for downloading from MSN, but you might have to pay a fee for downloading that application, just as you might pay to purchase the application from a computer software store.

Before you download a file in this lesson, you will check the file's properties to verify that it is free. Make sure you begin this lesson in MSN Central.

142 Project 7 Accessing The Microsoft Network

To Download a File from MSN

1 Click Categories.

The Categories window appears.

2 Choose Edit, Go To, Other Location.

The Edit menu drops down. This is a shortcut way to access certain information areas. Most files you download will be compressed. In this example, you will access the Computer Education BBS library to find a compression package so that you can download future offerings from MSN when you see them. The access word, or Go word for this service is **CEBBS**.

The Go To Service dialog box appears, which prompts you for the Go word.

3 Type CEBBS in the Type a Go Word For a Particular Service text box, and click OK (see Fig. 7.8).

MSN goes directly to the Computer Education File Library and opens it (see Fig. 7.9). The paper clip icon to the right of the arrow in each posting indicates that there is an attached file.

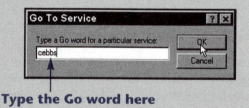

Figure 7.8
Use the Go To Service dialog box to save expense and time by going directly to your topic of interest.

Type the Go word here

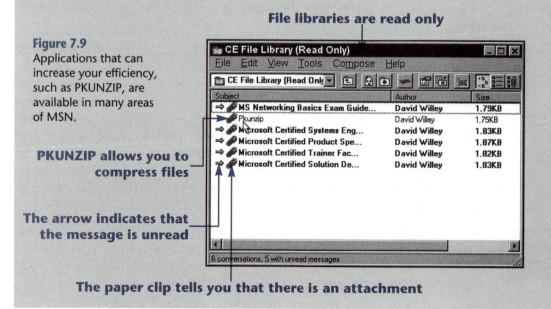

Figure 7.9
Applications that can increase your efficiency, such as PKUNZIP, are available in many areas of MSN.

File libraries are read only

PKUNZIP allows you to compress files

The arrow indicates that the message is unread

The paper clip tells you that there is an attachment

Lesson 3: Downloading a File from MSN 143

④ Double-click PKUNZIP to open that posting in the library.

You can also open a posting by right-clicking the file and selecting Open. A posting that looks similar to an e-mail message opens. It should include a brief description of the file available for downloading and an icon that represents the file you can download.

⑤ Right-click the file icon in the posting. When the shortcut menu appears, choose Properties.

The Properties dialog box appears for the attached file, as shown in Figure 7.10. The General tab informs you of the file size, download time, and price of the file. You can choose to download the file (without opening it), or download and open the program.

⑥ Click the Download and Open button.

The file downloads to your system and opens for future use. Your instructor might want you to run through the steps of using PKUNZIP now, so ask your instructor if you should close PKUNZIP to prepare for the next lesson.

⑦ Return to MSN Central.

Close any other windows you might have opened throughout this lesson in preparation for Lesson 5.

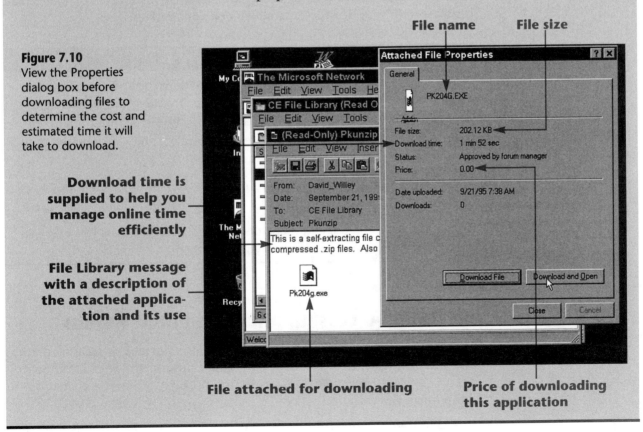

Figure 7.10
View the Properties dialog box before downloading files to determine the cost and estimated time it will take to download.

Download time is supplied to help you manage online time efficiently

File Library message with a description of the attached application and its use

File attached for downloading

File name   File size

Price of downloading this application

Jargon Watch

The online revolution created by the Internet, World Wide Web, and online services have produced many new terms you need to be aware of. In MSN, a **Go word** identifies a service to MSN so that it can directly access that service for you. You can find Go words in the Properties dialog box of any service.

Compressed files are files that have been reduced in size (the amount of space they take up on a computer or disk). **Compression utilities** are applications that are capable of compressing files. In online communications, it is a concern to navigate as efficiently as you can to save time, thereby saving online fees. Because of this, if you want to transfer a file, you want it to be compressed (or "zipped") so it will travel across modem lines quickly and shorten your amount of access time when sending that file. One of the most popular packages available for this is PKUNZIP.

You should always view the properties of a file before downloading it. View properties to find out the size of the file, the time it will take to transfer the file to your systems, and the fee for copying the file. Right-click the icon and select Properties to view the file properties.

If you do not check the properties, you can download a file to your system by double-clicking the file icon.

To quickly copy files to your desktop, just click a file icon to select it, and drag the file icon to your desktop or to a folder on your desktop.

If you have problems...

You can change compressed-file options for downloading if you need to control your access time. Choose **T**ools, File Transfer Status. This option allows for further file manipulation and opens the **F**ile Transfer Status window. Choose **T**ools, **O**ptions. Select or deselect the Compressed Files options you want to change.

If you want to always download your transferred files to a certain folder, in Options, type the path of the folder in the Default Download Folder box.

You can postpone the automatic decompression of the files. This way you can decompress them later when you need them.

Lesson 4: Accessing and Using Chat Rooms

The Microsoft Network is an excellent resource for accessing information and interacting with people and companies around the world. When you are in the MSN, you might see interesting postings or enter a chat room to jump into a conversation.

In a chat room, you can interact with others in real time. Just as the name implies, you can "chat" with others online when you are in a chat room. To participate, you just need to find a chat room that is holding a discussion

Lesson 4: Accessing and Using Chat Rooms   145

you are interested in, and begin sending or receiving messages. What you type in the chat area is seen immediately. At all times, you should stick to topics of interest to that particular chat. If you have any concerns about this, please refer to the Member Assistance area. In this lesson, you learn to find and interact with a chat group.

To Access and Use Chat Rooms

❶ Choose Tools, Find in MSN Central.

You can choose Tools, Find from anywhere in MSN. The Find dialog box opens. The cursor automatically appears in the Containing text box.

❷ Type the word Stock.

You can further limit your search, but for this exercise, no changes need to be made.

❸ Click the Find Now button.

MSN searches the network and returns all matching options, as shown in Figure 7.11. This is the best way to get around MSN. Use Find. Type the topic you are interested in, choose from the results, and post those results to your Favorite Places or create a shortcut to it on your desktop.

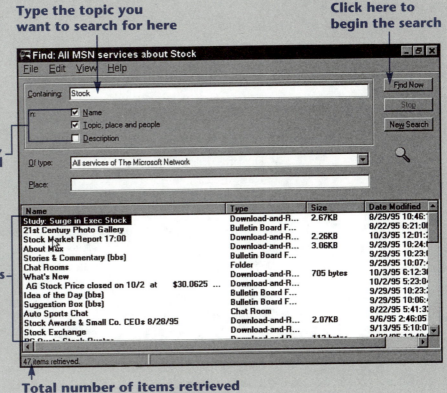

Figure 7.11
It is a good idea to use Find to search for all items available on the topic you want to view.

continues

To Access and Use Chat Rooms (continued)

4 **Double-click the search result Chat Rooms.**

Chats are dynamic. For that reason, the chat in Figure 7.12 will not exist for very long. Your instructor will guide you on which chat room to access in the chat room area. If your class enters an empty chat room, chat among yourselves.

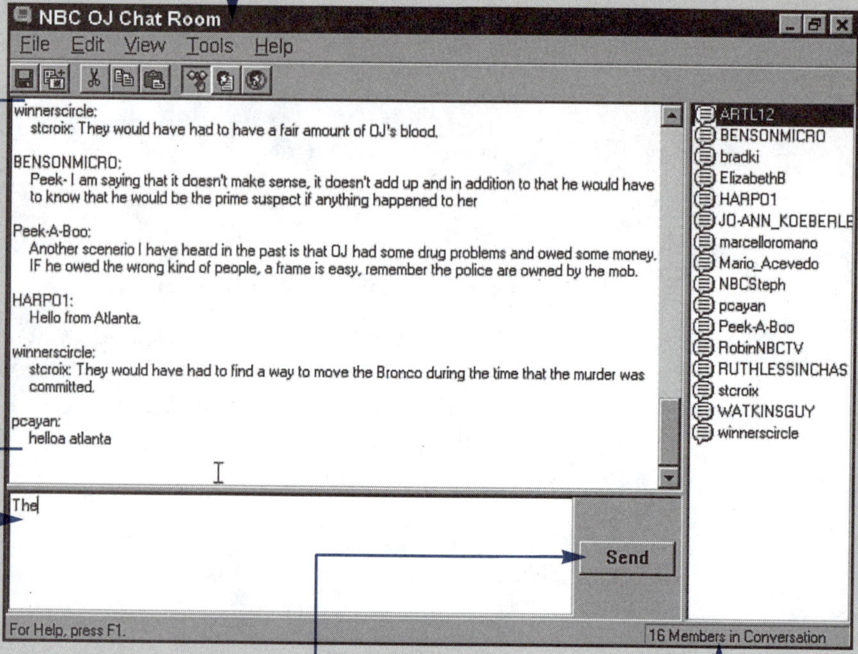

Chat name

Figure 7.12
This is an example of a chat in progress.

Actual live chat

Enter your message here

Click Send or press Enter to send your message

The total number of chat participants

5 **Type a message in the message area.**

Do not press ⏎Enter at this time. This will post the message. If you want a carriage return in your message, press Ctrl+⏎Enter.

6 **Click Send when you finish typing the message.**

In this lesson, you will use Send, but remember, you can also post your message by pressing ⏎Enter. It's not a good habit to get into, because then if you want a carriage return in your text, you might forget, hit ⏎Enter instead of Ctrl+⏎Enter, and post a partial message to the chat session. Your message appears instantly on the screen for others to read and reply to.

7 **Choose File, Exit.**

You exit the chat. Return to MSN Central.

Lesson 5: Accessing and Using Bulletin Board Services   147

Jargon Watch

Chat rooms consist of the people chatting, called **participants**, and people watching the session, called **spectators**. When you enter a chat, it might be a group of individuals in an unplanned format or it might be a chat session hosted by a designated guest. If a chat is hosted, it is usually by a BBS Forum Manager who has requested the use of the room through MSN to present a chat on a particular subject. The designated guest or forum manager guides the conversation and determines whether you want to participate or be a spectator. Chat rooms are open to anyone and are located throughout MSN. Type **chat** in the Find dialog box to see a listing.

Chats differ from Bulletin Board Services (BBSes) because BBSes usually have a Forum Manager to control the improper use of the forum and assist in answering inquiries. Chat room forum managers visit only to set up a chat. BBSes can also contain File Libraries, such as the one you saw earlier with the Computer Education BBS. Chats and e-mails have neither a designated Forum Manager nor file libraries.

Lesson 5: Accessing and Using Bulletin Board Services

BBS messages are not in real time. You post a message or reply to a message, and the message appears shortly after you type it. The delay is a very short amount of time.

Messages are retained in the BBS for viewing at any time. You can see messages by conversational thread or in the order they are posted. Different views are also available. Feel free to ask or answer questions, or to express your opinion on the topic of that BBS.

To Access and Use a Bulletin Board Service

A **shortcut** icon in The Microsoft Network lets you go to a different location without having to follow queues from MSN Central through each category to arrive at the same service or function the shortcut goes to. You can right-click the icon and choose Activate Shortcut to activate the object. You can also activate an object by simply double-clicking the object.

❶ In MSN Central, choose Edit, Go To, Other Location.

You can use Go To from most locations in MSN. In previous lessons, you also accessed areas by double-clicking the icon of interest. You can use either method. The Go To method saves online time and expense. The Go To Service dialog box appears.

❷ Type edTechBBS.

This is the Go word for the Computer Education BBS.

❸ Click OK or press ⏎Enter to access the Computer Education BBS.

The Computer Education BBS opens. This, too, is a constantly changing area. You can view postings by conversation thread, date posted, or other sorting criteria. It is best for the novice user to work with conversation threads because it is easier to follow the conversation.

continues

148 Project 7 Accessing The Microsoft Network

To Access and Use a Bulletin Board Service (continued)

4 Double-click a message to activate that message.

Your instructor can advise you which message to open. When you're in a BBS, you can double-click any message to open and read the message. The posting appears on your screen to read. If that posting has a **shortcut**, you can activate the shortcut. But the screen provides several other options when communicating on a BBS. Try these options now in the BBS.

5 Click the Close button.

Remain in the BBS for the next steps.

To Create or Reply to a BBS Posting

1 Click Compose in the Computer Education BBS.

A drop-down menu appears with options for composing a new message or replying to a message. Both actions are similar to your Inbox procedures. If you want to reply to a message, such as the message you opened in the previous steps, just click the Reply button instead of following steps 1 and 2.

2 Select New Message.

An e-mail message appears with all the e-mail toolbar icons you are familiar with.

3 Type your message or response to the original posting.

Click the Send button. Your posting appears in the BBS with the next update. Postings can sometimes appear quickly, even though the items are being posted to a BBS. However, for an immediate, real-time conversation, the Chat Room is most effective. You return to the BBS window.

4 Click the Up or Down arrows in a posting.

This will bring you to the previous or next posting without leaving the posting screen.

Lesson 6: Browsing Internet Newsgroups

Access to Internet Newsgroups is available in MSN. The Internet connects millions of computers around the world, providing content, answers, and topics of interest to particular groups of people. In this lesson, you cover Internet-access features you might need when working in MSN. The Internet Newsgroups contain BBSes like MSN BBSes, except that any user on the Internet can respond. For this reason, you might be blocked from Internet access through your company in order to maintain corporate security.

Lesson 7: Disconnecting from The Microsoft Network   149

To Browse Internet Newsgroups

1 Return to MSN Central.

You can return by clicking the MSN Central button on the toolbar.

2 Click Categories.

The variety of categories appears.

3 Double-click the Internet Center icon.

The Internet Center opens in a window. Read these postings in the same way you read the Bulletin Board postings to get a feel for the tone of the Newsgroup before actually posting a message.

Try the Internet icon in MSN's Member Assistance. There are Internet experts here to answer your questions about the Internet and how to interact.

Table 7.2 describes how to perform basic functions in a BBS. Use the BBS to become familiar with basic procedures.

Table 7.2 How Tos in a BBS

How to	Response
Copy files to Internet Newsgroups	MSN can't copy files directly to Internet Newsgroups.
Forum Managers	You can contact a Forum Manager by e-mail if you want to make a suggestion, report a problem, or discuss other matters.
Discern new and old messages	New messages that have not yet been read appear in bold type.
Follow a thread	In Conversation view (available from the toolbar), you can see a subject and follow the responses in a coherent manner.
Get just new messages	In List view, you can see items you have not yet read listed together in bold print.
See only file attachments	Use Attachment view.
Upload a file to a BBS	Contact the Forum Manager by e-mail and explain your request.

Lesson 7: Disconnecting from The Microsoft Network

In this project, you learned how to access The Microsoft Network, and to communicate with others using BBS postings and chat rooms. More importantly, you can download files and create shortcuts to enhance your performance at both the office and when communicating with people from home. Now you can disconnect from The Microsoft Network using the following instructions.

150 Project 7 Accessing The Microsoft Network

To Disconnect from The Microsoft Network

❶ From any location in The Microsoft Network, choose File, Sign Out.

This informs Microsoft Network that you want to disconnect. You are prompted to verify that it is OK to disconnect from The Microsoft Network.

❷ Click OK.

The Microsoft Network disconnects, the modem disconnects, and you can continue working on your computer as you have been.

Project Summary

To	Do This
Access MSN	Double-click MSN desktop icon, type member ID and Password; click Connect.
Access MSN Today	Click MSN Today button; click any item in the MSN Today screen.
Access Favorite Places	Click Favorite Places button; double-click the icon you want.
Access Member Assistance	Click Member Assistance button; double-click the icon you want.
Access Categories	Click Categories button; double-click the icon you want.
View MSN with Explorer	Open any folder with a right-click; choose Explore.
Download a file	Double-click the file icon.
Access an item with a Go word	Choose Edit, Go To, Other Location; type the Go word, click OK.
Check file properties	Right-click the file icon; choose Properties.
Find an item	Choose Tools, Find; type the word; click Find Now.
Post a chat message	Type the message in the Create area and click Send.
Read a BBS message	Double-click the message.
Reply to a BBS message	Choose Compose, choose how you want to reply; type the message; click Send.
Compose a new message in a BBS	Choose Compose, New Message; type the message; click Send.
Create shortcut to an MSN location	Right-click the icon, click Create Shortcut.

Applying Your Skills

1. Open The Microsoft Network; pick up your e-mail.

2. Go to the Member Assistance area and browse the Lobby Newsstand.

3. Find all topics on Word for Windows and Office 95.

4. Go to the Computer Education File Library using the Go word and, with permission from your Systems Administrator, download PKUNZIP for future use.

5. Put the icons you will need in your Favorite Places folder or on your desktop as shortcuts.